W9-BNC-098

You Get Past the Tears

VILLARD ⓥ NEW YORK

You Get Past the Tears

A Memoir of Love and Survival

PATRICIA BROADBENT
AND HYDEIA BROADBENT

with Patricia Romanowski

Foreword by Philip A. Pizzo, M.D.

OUACHITA TECHNICAL COLLEGE

All rights reserved under International and Pan-American
Copyright Conventions. Published in the United States by
Villard Books, a division of Random House, Inc., New York,
and simultaneously in Canada by Random House
of Canada Limited, Toronto.

Villard Books is a registered trademark of Random House, Inc.
Colophon is a trademark of Random House, Inc.

All photographs in this book, unless otherwise credited, are from the
authors' collection.

Library of Congress Cataloging-in-Publication data is available.

ISBN 0-679-46314-3

Villard Books website address: www.villard.com
Printed in the United States of America on acid-free paper

2 4 6 8 9 7 5 3

First Edition

Book design by Jo Anne Metsch

DEDICATION

To my children Kendall, Pepe, Kimmie, and Patricia, for unselfishly going the extra miles in ways too numerous to describe. Your unconditional love of family enabled us to journey this far together.

To my daughter Keisha: You always understood and remembered that I love you, despite my absences and the times you missed a mother's presence.

To my mother, for inspiring me and for providing a living example of strength, courage, and perseverance.

To the memories of the first children who went on protocol but ultimately lost their struggle. Because of their courage and their parents' dedication to expanding our knowledge of pediatric AIDS, children like Hydeia and Patricia were given a better chance.

PATRICIA BROADBENT

FOREWORD:
GIVING A VOICE AND FACE
TO PEDIATRIC AIDS

*F*or the pediatric community the 1980s were hallmarked by the emergence of a frightening and devastating new illness impacting children and their families. Children from racial and ethnic minorities or from families suffering from poverty were disproportionately affected. To many the new disease, called acquired immunodeficiency syndrome (AIDS), caused by a virus identified as the human immunodeficiency virus (HIV), represented a cause for alarm, being characterized by a rising incidence, a high mortality, and a nearly nonexistent therapeutic arsenal.

At the time that the first cases of AIDS and HIV infection in children were described, I was at the National Cancer Institute in Bethesda, Maryland. My research group there, where I had worked since 1973, had been focused on improving the care and treatment of children with cancer through biomedical research. We had considerable experience in the study and development of new drugs and the approach to complex medical problems. Moreover, I had expertise in pediatric oncology as well as infectious disease, and thus felt that our program had both the skills and the responsibility to try to combat this new disease. Accordingly, I made the decision in 1985 that we would begin a new research program in pediatric AIDS at the Clinical Center of the National Institutes of Health.

I did not anticipate, however, the vast array of both medical and nonmedical challenges we would face in caring for children with this new disease. These included the anxieties of our own medical and nursing staff; the fears and discrimination of our communities, schools, and society; the lack of support for pediatric research; and the obstacles to drug development for children. Indeed, many of these obstacles were dramatically different from what I had encountered in my research into and care for children with cancer, where concern and compassion seemed to be the norm.

Part of the reason for these fears and anxieties was the faceless and voiceless nature of this new, rapidly emerging fatal illness. Hydeia Broadbent helped to change that by giving it a face and a voice that spoke to and for children and their parents. It was a voice that was sounded in song, verse, and spoken words, well beyond Hydeia's chronological age of five years. It conveyed messages that could not be ignored because they evoked compassion and wisdom, honesty and expectation. Hydeia and her mother, Pat, became advocates for change, a clarion for a future generation of children.

It is remarkable how children can alter one's knowledge and shatter preconceived myths. Although I had been caring for children with life-threatening diseases for more than a decade when we began our work with pediatric AIDS, I was unprepared for the wisdom that even young children could shed on their own illness and its impact on siblings, parents, and friends. Dr. Lori Wiener, a social worker of extraordinary ability and insight, provided the vehicles and instruments for children, including Hydeia, that permitted them to use their voices so they could tell us what it meant and felt like to face the challenge of AIDS.

Through their stories, poems, drawings, and, in Hydeia's case, spontaneous songs and conversation, written, collated, and videotaped by Dr. Wiener, we were challenged to listen and learn. Hydeia, even at five and six years of age, possessed an extraordinary ability to describe how it felt to have AIDS, what it meant to have acquired it from a mother who had used drugs, how appreciative she was to have been adopted by Pat Broadbent, and how much she was counting on us, all of us, to do something about the disease that impacted her and her friends. She indeed gave a voice and face to this illness.

The impact of Hydeia, as a patient and as an advocate, coupled with the remarkable dedication and commitment of her adoptive parents, especially Pat, cannot be stated strongly enough. Hydeia won over even the most frightened and made society listen. Initially this was a local phenomenon, within our programs at the NIH, but soon it became more public and then national, as Hydeia became a public personality, a child spokesperson for pediatric AIDS. I worried about the impact of an emerging public life on a child facing a serious illness but recognized that Pat's care and protection enabled Hydeia to speak out without losing her childhood and her sense of hope.

For those fortunate enough to not have to experience a significant illness, to not have to watch a child suffer the ravages of a disease and the prospect of death, to not see the suffering and loss of family or the limitations of medical research and therapy, it is important to be reminded that disease can change a life forever. Words can help us to understand this, but they are much more powerfully expressed when spoken by a child. The story of Hydeia and Pat Broadbent told in *You Get Past the Tears* is one of survival, of being unwilling to accept "no" or the idea that progress cannot be made. It is a message of survival but also of advocacy. It is a story of how public opinion can be changed and the course of a ravaging illness altered.

Just a decade ago it seemed clear that our country would have an ever-growing number of children with AIDS. They would all have voices and faces, perhaps not as articulate or captivating as Hydeia's, but they would each represent a life challenged and potentially lost. Because of the work of Hydeia and Pat, their personal sacrifices, their willingness to participate in clinical trials testing new drugs and agents for children with AIDS, their commitment to speaking out for additional research dollars, more drug trials, more compassion, and improved care, the face of pediatric AIDS in the United States and developed countries has been dramatically changed. The research programs that were spawned in the 1980s paved the way for treatments that could prevent the transmission of HIV from mother to child. If born today, Hydeia might not have become infected with HIV.

But looking back is not what Hydeia or Pat Broadbent have spent their lives doing. They have been looking forward, working hard to move beyond the tears so that they can celebrate the lives they have and help make better ones for children in the future. And their efforts are still all too needed.

As a pediatric specialist for nearly three decades, I have interacted with many children and many families facing a life-threatening disease. Each has had an impact on me personally. Some have had an impact on society as well. Hydeia falls into this latter category. Regardless of what comes next, her life is measured by the smiles and laughter she has brought to others, by the accounting she has demanded of what truly matters, by her expectations that we take her and her illness seriously and, most important, do something about it.

I will always remember Hydeia and forever be grateful to have known her, admired her, and learned from her. *You Get Past the Tears* is a story of courage, strength, wisdom, and love. It is a reminder that children can teach us much about who we are, why we exist, and what really counts in life.

PHILIP A. PIZZO, M.D.
Carl and Elizabeth Naumann Professor of Pediatrics
and of Microbiology and Immunology
Dean, Stanford University School of Medicine

ACKNOWLEDGMENTS

Over the course of this journey, my family and I have crossed paths with thousands of other men, women, and children whose lives were touched by pediatric AIDS. In addition to the children and families we got to know through our visits to the National Institutes of Health and our various travels, we have also met affected families and legions of dedicated people through our participation with other AIDS support and education organizations and events. It would be impossible to list everyone here by name. In addition, there were moments when the kind word, gesture, or deed that saved my sanity or my daughter's life came from someone whose name I never learned. To every one of these people, I extend my sincere and heartfelt thanks.

I would like to thank all of the doctors, nurses, technicians, and other medical personnel whose hard work and devotion gave my daughters Hydeia and Patricia, as well as millions of other children, the gift of life. First among them is Dr. Philip A. Pizzo and his team at the National Institutes of Health, not only for treating the children stricken by AIDS but also for taking such good care of parents and families. Our social worker at NIH, Lori Wiener, had a smile on her face the first day I met her, and that smile has never dimmed. Her willingness to help and her genuine concern for our family remains steadfast. In Lori I found not only a caring professional but a shoulder to cry on and a wonderful friend. Trish Scullion did so much for Hydeia and me that she became part of our family. Closer to home, Harlene Farrell, R.N., worked and traveled with Hydeia and me for more than twelve years and was always here to help. I would also like to thank Dr. Bruce Ogden here in Las Vegas.

The support and understanding of family and friends remain crucial. I wish to thank especially my lifelong best friend, Rita Lewis, for doing more than just being there. If a friend in need is a friend indeed, I was a friend for sure. She listened to me for hours and has helped in so many ways. Cindy Small reached out to me from the very beginning and has since shared so many steps with me. I thank her and her family for all of their support. I would also like to acknowledge my brothers and sisters: Ursula, Walter, Judy, Gerard, Rita, and Joyce.

Thank you to Bill and Claire Milligan for starting the Hydeia L. Broadbent Foundation and for your special friendship. Thank you, Delores and Conrad Bullard, for your dedication in continuing to run the foundation and your commitment to seeing it grow. We are truly family now. Thanks to my mentor, the Reverend Dr. Barbara King, for your wisdom and friendship. You hold a special place in my heart.

More recent friends who deserve acknowledgment for their efforts on our family's behalf are David Reynoso and Deborah Langford. I would also like to acknowledge everyone at the Elizabeth Glaser Pediatric AIDS Foundation, with whom I feel a special bond, and Neil Willenson and the staff at Camp Heartland.

It had never occurred to me to write a book, and it took a while to convince me I had something to say. I thank my editor, Melody Guy, at Villard for her persistence, for believing in this project, and for understanding that the story I wanted to tell was not so much about AIDS as about parenthood. My literary agent, Sarah Lazin, helped me to see that I did have a story to tell, and even before we met in person, I considered her a friend. My cowriter, Patty Romanowski, was both determined and patient. She made me remember things I'd have been just as happy to forget, but I also enjoyed our conversations. I would also like to thank Karen Hunter for the time and effort she devoted in the early stages of the project.

Finally, I thank the hundreds of other people who have been so generous to us through the years. That your name may not appear on these pages in no way diminishes your importance or our appreciation.

PATRICIA BROADBENT

In addition to the people my mother has thanked, I would also like to acknowledge all of my brothers and sisters, for supporting me, for being there, and for loving me. Especially my sister Keisha, who probably missed my mom most when she was taking care of me. I'd like to thank my dad for being there for me. Also, thank you to the Hill family, who are like my second family, and to my best friend, Sonya, for talking to me when I was going crazy. Finally, I wish to acknowledge all of the friends I have made during my life, none of whom I will ever forget.

HYDEIA BROADBENT

I am the future, and I have AIDS. I am Hydeia L. Broadbent. I can do anything I put my mind to. I'm the next
doctor. I'm the next lawyer. I'm the next Maya Angelou.
I might even be the first woman president. You can't
crush my dreams.

—*My daughter, addressing the*
1996 Republican National
Convention, San Diego

*L*ong before a child's first words or first steps, we naturally
wonder who she might grow up to be, where she might go, what
she might do. Years before she can dream for herself, we dream
for her: of happy days, special accomplishments, and moments
to cherish. We say, "When she grows up," never doubting that
she will. We assume that our love and protection will deflect the
hard knocks we know lie in wait for everyone. *But not my child,*
we tell ourselves. *Not my child.*

The story I'm going to tell you is not the kind of story any
mother imagines having to tell. I know I never thought I would.
In late 1984 my husband, Loren, and I chose a baby girl named
Hydeia to join four older children in our family. We knew we
could give her a better chance at life. We were confident that we
could provide the love, support, protection, and guidance all
children need and deserve. We were certain that for Hydeia, who
had been abandoned in the hospital at birth by a mother ad-
dicted to drugs, the life we could give her could only be better.
First as her foster parent, I silently promised her a loving home.

Once we decided to adopt her, I made that leap of faith that all parents make, no matter how their children come to them. I vowed to love, protect, and shelter her. I would make a difference.

In the spring of 1988, when Hydeia was just a few months short of four, reality shattered my confidence in my power to protect her. We learned that Hydeia had been infected with HIV at birth. Although, technically speaking, she had not yet developed AIDS, at a time when there were no HIV treatments available to children the prognosis was certain: She probably would not live much beyond her fifth birthday.

It is now more than twelve years later. Not only is Hydeia still here, she is also an internationally recognized AIDS activist and, even more remarkably, a typical teenager. She is among the first generation of children with AIDS for whom science has changed the odds—the first generation for whom adulthood is a possibility and not just a dream. This is the story of how we got from that dark day in 1988 to today.

Since the early 1990s, when media exposure made Hydeia one of the most widely recognized "faces" of pediatric AIDS, she and our family have been the subjects of countless television programs, documentaries, and articles. It would be easy to tell our story in clichés about miracles and hope, tragedy and the "innocent" victims of the epidemic. I know, too, how easy it is to view Hydeia, myself, and our family as somehow "special." The truth is, however, we are a family just like any other. I am no stronger or braver than any other mother who loves her child. All I have done is everything in my power to defy that first hopeless prognosis. As you will see, the fact that Hydeia is in most respects a typical teenager is in itself nothing short of a miracle. It would be wrong, however, not to point out that this was a miracle made by many hands, and a miracle that owes its existence to some turns of fate we could have easily missed.

Yes, this is a story about devastation, struggle, and loss. It is also a story of love, commitment, and hope. More important, though, it is not just a story about our family. It is the story of a disease that is still infecting and killing far more children and adults than it should. For Hydeia and her younger sister, Patricia, who also has AIDS, there was no choice, perhaps not even for their birth mothers, who passed the virus on to them. But now, more than twenty years after the virus was first identified, after more than 700,000 Americans have developed AIDS and more than 440,000 have died—including more than 5,000 children under fifteen—it does come down to the choices each of us makes every single day. Sixty-three percent of the children living with AIDS today are African-American; another 25 percent are Hispanic. For the vast majority of adolescents and adults who become newly infected with HIV, the tragedy lies not only in their being infected but also in the fact that in most cases they did not have to be. The vast majority of infected children—over 90 percent of all pediatric HIV and AIDS cases contract the virus before or at birth—"inherit" the consequences of one or both parents' choices.

Back in the late 1980s, when I first began speaking out about AIDS, ignorance and fear ran rampant. Not a week went by when you didn't hear of children being denied access to school or adults losing their jobs, their homes, even their families, because they had AIDS. When it became clear that there were ways to lower the risk of contracting or spreading HIV, the focus shifted. For Hydeia, who has been speaking publicly about HIV and AIDS since the age of six, the message has always been about acceptance of those who have the disease and making the right choices to help stop its spread.

When I first agreed to allow Hydeia to speak out about AIDS, I viewed it as a "temporary job." I honestly believed that after a few years, her work would be done. Considering all that's at stake, I couldn't imagine that people would not embrace the information Hydeia and others have offered to help us all make the choices that could finally stop this killer. Yet here we are at the dawn of the twenty-first century, and HIV is infecting some groups of people—particularly black and minority women and children—at higher rates than before. For example, while African-Americans represent only 12 percent of the U.S. population, they account for 37 percent of all AIDS cases, 62 percent of all AIDS cases among women, and 62 percent of all pediatric AIDS cases. Half of all new HIV infections in the United States are among people under twenty-five. Only a minority of adolescents who have HIV are aware that they are infected. That means that those with whom they have intimate sexual contact or share needles are being infected. It also means that despite the ability to decrease dramatically the chances that an infected mother will pass HIV on to her unborn child, babies will continue to be born with HIV, just like Hydeia.

Yes, the medications and the treatments have improved. Yes, some people with AIDS are living longer lives, and in many ways better lives, than ever before. However, the key word there is *some*. Not everyone can take these lifesaving miracle drugs. And even for those who can, AIDS never truly goes away. There is no cure for AIDS today, and there may not be tomorrow, either. It is still a killer. We seem so dazzled by the bright, happy headlines of "breakthroughs" and "miracle" stories, we seem to have lost sight of this. As I look at the people who come to hear Hydeia speak, I often wonder if her poise, her healthy appearance, and her positive personality do not obscure, in their eyes, the reality of living with AIDS. Do they really know what it means to spend your life trying to outwit and outrun this persistent and wily killer? Do they understand that for every child like Hydeia, there are thousands of others who lost the fight, among them her friends? Do they realize that for Hydeia and others who are infected with HIV, there is no rest from this race, no moment you can drop your guard or lower your vigilance? All it takes is one cough that doesn't sound quite right, one lab report that deviates from the expected, or another child's passing to remind us that this ain't over yet. AIDS has many tricks up its sleeve, and I'm not foolish enough to think we have seen them all.

The story of AIDS today is not so much about the amazing things we have learned as it is about the very basic facts we seem to have forgotten. We seem to have forgotten that every year or two brings a new generation of babies, children, and young adults from whom this virus continues to exact a terrible toll. Like the virus itself, our ignorance about it seems to have mutated, shifted, and changed. We may no longer suffer from the early fear of those with HIV or AIDS, but we now have complacency; in place of horror, we now have denial.

For more than a decade Hydeia has traveled the country spreading her message about AIDS. In the process, she has touched the hearts and the minds of millions. She has changed the way many people see this disease and, more important, the way they view those who have it. She has saved lives, inspired acceptance, and taught lessons of responsibility and compassion to people many times her age. Organizations around the world have recognized Hydeia as a leader and a hero of her generation. Through it all, however, she has also remained in many ways a typical young woman who does what she does because she sees more clearly than most people why it matters.

Though this book tells our story, it is not simply a book about Hydeia and our family. What happened to Hydeia and to us could happen to anyone. And it does. Even as you read this, there is a baby being born infected, a teenager trading a few minutes' carelessness for a lifetime of heartache. We hope that in our story you will find the inspiration to make the choices today that ensure that AIDS will not become part of your story, your family's story, or your children's stories tomorrow.

PATRICIA BROADBENT

You Get Past the Tears

ONE

The first time I saw her, she didn't even have a real name.

Just six weeks old, she had been taken from the hospital nursery, where her mother had abandoned her, to Child Haven, a county-run temporary facility. Now, here at my doorstep, was Baby Girl Kelloggs. As it turned out, Kelloggs was not her father's name or her mother's, either. Perhaps her mother picked it up off a cereal box. This fact, like so many I learned about the children I had fostered or adopted over the years, would have shocked me if I hadn't heard a dozen stories like it before, and worse. A veteran social worker, an activist for minority adoptions, and a foster parent, I knew how this story began and how it would probably end. A baby born to a drug-addicted mother and temporarily cared for by the state now needed a loving home until she could be adopted. A friend who worked for the state had called and told me about this baby. Was I interested in taking care of her until she could be adopted? As a foster parent, my role in this little one's life would be brief but, I hoped, important. Having taken in several foster children before, I had learned the art of loving and caring for children who would not be mine forever. I knew when to hold tight and when to let go, how to draw the lines around my heart and theirs so that they regarded me as Auntie Pat and not Mommy. (Besides, I already had four of my own children to call me Mom.)

This little one, like so many, was born with drugs in her system. That, along with the fact that her mother had left the hospital within hours of giving birth, told me that she probably had not received good prenatal care. I expected a baby who was smaller than average, more likely to fuss, less likely to interact spontaneously. I wouldn't have been surprised if she had problems with eating and sleeping or didn't like to be held as much as other babies. That was okay. To hear the media—then in the grip of hysteria over crack babies—tell it, "drug babies" were close to hopeless. But I knew better. With a few months' care, love, and attention, this baby girl would blossom. Even before she arrived, I was looking forward to the day when she would leave in the arms of adoptive parents who would love her forever.

If this sounds a little idealistic, then maybe I was, even though I have always been a very pragmatic person. Some people see taking in a foster child as a noble sacrifice. For me it wasn't about that. I had always enjoyed kids and had spent most of my adult life working with them in both the public and private sectors. I imagine that there were people who looked at the lifestyle my husband, Loren, and I had made and wondered why we did it. Three children from my previous marriage and one from ours had been adopted. I had always felt that parenting had more to do with how you raised a child once you got him than with how you got him.

By the time this little baby girl came along, two of my children, Paige, or Pepe, as we called him, and Kimmie, were teenagers. My oldest son, Kendall, was an adult, married and stationed in Germany with the military. We had decided that our family was complete. There would be no more adoptions, but that didn't stop me from wanting to help a child however I could. Most of the children we fostered were thrown into the system because their parents—usually their mothers, since fathers were rarely involved—could not care for them, for various reasons. Sometimes, as in the case of this little one, the parent made it clear enough through her actions that there would be no going "home." For many others, however, there was hope. There were mothers and fathers who worked very hard to overcome the obstacles that kept them from being the parents their kid deserved. It felt good to provide a safe, temporary home until parents could take a child back. Recalling the positive life-long impressions a few caring adults had made on me as a kid, I truly believed that I could and did make a difference. When we brought foster children into our home, we made them feel at home. I knew of some foster families who would send the foster kids to another foster home while they went off on vacation. We didn't believe that was right. Wherever we went, they went. We provided extra clothes and toys—items that were not covered by the small monthly payment we received for their care.

Even after you explain all that, some people still wonder why you do it. At the time, I was the unit director of a Boys Club of America chapter and the executive director of Camp Fire Girls. Those jobs, like most I'd had throughout my career, involved helping kids and providing a role model. I guess you could say that I gave at the office but felt the need to do more. Financially and emotionally, I could do more. We were financially secure and upwardly mobile, with a six-figure income, a new car every couple of years, and a Mercedes out in the double garage. With Las Vegas on the verge of a major boom, we had amassed a healthy portfolio of real estate that practically guaranteed we could retire around age fifty. In the meantime, though, we didn't sweat it. If we saw something we wanted, we bought it. If there was somewhere we wanted to vacation, we went. After years of moving from one side of the country to the other because of my first husband's military career, I was ready to settle down. I felt that I'd finally found the partner, the lifestyle, and the home I had dreamed of. To have come to this place and yet still be in my early forties struck me as some kind of blessing. Every which way you cut it, we had it made.

It was mid-July, and it was hot, even for Las Vegas. My friend Luria Walker, who worked for the Nevada Division of Welfare, had called to say she was bringing the baby over. When she pulled up in front of our house and tooted her horn, I hurried outside. As I leaned in and reached for the baby in the backseat, I couldn't believe how tiny she was. Not only that, her skin was still wrinkled, just like a newborn's. Weighing under six pounds (less than what she had weighed at birth), this baby looked more like she was six *days* old. At six weeks, she should have regained her birth weight plus at least another pound.

"Are you sure this is the baby?" I asked Luria. "She looks like she was just born!"

"Yeah, this is her," Luria replied.

"Gosh, she's so little," I said, noticing that the orange-and-white Cabbage Patch outfit she wore wasn't a baby-size version of the popular dolls' clothing—it was a pajama set literally made for a doll. She was that tiny. Her complexion was chocolate, and with her fine, straight black hair and delicate features, she looked almost East Indian. All she was missing, I would joke, was a red dot on her forehead. With her big brown eyes and fine black hair, she was a very pretty baby.

The idea of having a baby girl in the family, even if only temporarily, really appealed to our youngest, three-year-old Briana, whom we call Keisha. There was a big age difference between Keisha and her older siblings, so in many ways she was essentially an only child. We found that taking in foster children not only helped them and their families but gave Keisha an opportunity to be around other kids and to learn to share. At the time, two brothers were living with us. Keisha liked them well enough, but she loved the idea of having a baby sister, and this was the first female foster child we ever had.

Oddly enough, that same day Keisha happened to watch an episode of *Sesame Street* that concerned a family having a baby. Every now and then, *Sesame Street* explores an important issue using the human characters or other real people without the Muppets. This program showed a mother discussing a new baby's arrival with a little girl not much older than Keisha. She told her, as I had told Keisha, that she would be a "big sister" and reassured her that there would be enough love for everyone. That made an impression on Keisha. The parents on *Sesame Street* gave their daughter a Swahili name—Hydeia (pronounced hie-DEE-uh), which means "again."

"Mommy, this is just like us!" Keisha said. "Can we name our baby Hydeia?"

"We sure can," I replied, pleased at how well Keisha was handling the new arrival. Of course, I didn't bother then to remind Keisha of the ways in which this new arrival was not like the one on television—namely, that this baby would not be staying. We had already discussed that, and I knew she understood that in a month we would bring Hydeia to an "adoption fair," where, we hoped, a loving couple would discover her. I remembered back when my eldest son, Kendall, then six, was determined to name his younger brother after himself. We gently explained to him that Kendall Paige Jr. would be a great name for *his* son, but that his brother needed something different. We compromised with Paige Bendall, though we always called him Pepe. Although I had never heard the name Hydeia before, it sounded both beautiful and strong, ancient yet new. It could have been the name of a warrior princess or wise woman. To grow up a smart, strong black woman in this world, I knew she would have to be a little of both. So she became Hydeia.

Of course, everyone in the house fussed over the baby. I still couldn't get over how tiny she was. As we soon learned, however, her size was the least of her problems. Babies are supposed to be hungry, and while I knew some feeding problems were par for the course with drug babies like Hydeia, this was something else. Most of what she ate either came right back up or gave her diarrhea. To look at her, you would think she was starving, yet she had no interest in eating. And this was the first baby I'd seen who was almost completely inconsolable. Everything about Hydeia was a contradiction: She was very weak but at the same time surprisingly alert. You could be holding her and she'd look so peaceful, then suddenly start screaming and crying for no apparent reason. The more you tried to comfort her by holding her or rocking her, the more she screamed. *Okay,* I told myself, *she's a drug baby. She'll be okay once she settles in.*

Though I knew what to expect, I sensed something wasn't right. If you had written a description of Hydeia and shown it to someone who worked with kids like her, they might say that it fit a baby with her history. However, to see it play out in real life, you knew there was something else. The first night, I expected to hear her cry. When I woke up at around five in the morning, I thought she was still sleeping. Once I got close enough to her bassinet, I realized she *was* crying. It was a barely audible, almost kittenish "Eh, eh, eh." She was that weak.

The next day I took her to see our family pediatrician, Dr. G. He took one look at her and, in a tone of disbelief bordering on annoyance, asked, "Why did you wait so long to bring her in?" I explained that I'd just gotten her yesterday and ran down the little bit of her history that I knew. I'm sure he was as puzzled as I was by the fact that at this age, Hydeia weighed less than she did at birth and no one at Child Haven seemed to have noticed. This was unusual, even for a drug baby, and I had called Child Haven and asked, "How can you have had this baby for six weeks and not taken her to a doctor?" Whatever answer I got, it

wasn't good enough. Dr. G. suggested that we switch her formula and see if that helped.

We changed formula, but nothing changed for Hydeia. So we
changed again, and again, and again. My sister Joyce was staying with us at the time, and we would take turns getting up at
night to feed Hydeia. She ate so little at each feeding, we had to
feed her more often. Even with the formula changes and using
every trick we knew, she still brought back up most of what she
did eat, and the diarrhea continued. When she broke into a sudden screaming fit, I found that placing her alone in her bassinet
was the best thing to do. Though she cried for a few minutes afterward, Hydeia seemed to do a better job of calming herself
down than we could.

The month passed quickly, and though we all understood that
Hydeia couldn't stay with us, she had become part of the family.
Loren and I had already decided that adopting her was out of
the question, and we prepared for the upcoming adoption fair
with every intention of one day soon packing up her tiny clothes
and saying good-bye.

Through my work in social services, I had seen firsthand the
difficulties experienced by children who, for whatever reason,
did not find permanent homes early on. In adoption lingo, "difficult to place" describes any child who is not a healthy white in-
fant. Once children grow beyond the "cute" baby stage or show
any indication of potential problems, they are less attractive to
most prospective adoptive parents. When I say "most," however, I want to be clear. There are adoptive parents who see beyond the complicated issues and potential problems to focus on
the child. To them, the mission is helping a child in need, not
simply finding the "perfect" child. They understand that any
child—including the one you give birth to—can be a challenge.
They know that life offers no guarantees. There are others,
however, who approach adoption with a list of specific requirements. For the vast majority of them, any disability or situa-

tion that might produce problems automatically eliminates a child from the "competition." A child who had been "in the system"—in other words, in foster care or in a place like Child Haven—"too long" also faced the very real possibility of remaining in the foster system and perhaps moving from family to family until adulthood. Those of us who worked with kids like these knew that in most cases these were good, resilient kids who just needed support, understanding, and patience.

Having adopted three children, I felt very strongly about the issue and sat on the board of an organization called Members and Advocates for Minority Adoption (MAMA). People who worked in the juvenile court system and in all types of social services made up the MAMA board. We were determined to level the playing field for these kids. To that end, we held an annual adoption fair, where prospective adoptive parents could meet the children in a setting more pleasant and relaxed than the local welfare office. There were clowns, games, balloons, and refreshments. It gave the older kids a chance to play and be themselves and, we felt, to make a more positive and realistic first impression.

This year the fair was held in the gymnasium of Las Vegas High School. As I dressed Hydeia for the event, I remember thinking how happy I would be if a young couple fell in love with her like we had. I knew that moment would be difficult, because I had long ago broken the first rule of foster care: "Love, but don't fall in love." I was in love with Hydeia but realistic. Loving her would require letting her go. My sister Joyce, who is a talented seamstress, had made Hydeia a special outfit for the day: matching dress, panties, hat, and booties of mint green cotton printed with tiny purple flowers. Joyce trimmed everything in delicate white eyelet lace and made a matching mint-and-purple blanket. As Loren, Keisha, and I found a place among the other foster parents, babies, and children, I knew Hydeia was, hands down, the prettiest baby there.

Hydeia sat in her baby carrier atop a counter, and Loren stayed there with her while I walked around talking to social worker friends. Loren understood what the adoption fair was all about, but he wasn't prepared for what happened. I guess he had expected a parade of smiling would-be parents cooing over Hydeia and instantly falling in love. Instead, he was surprised by the intense curiosity in Hydeia's racial background and taken aback by the directness with which people asked, "What is she, anyway?" and "Is she mixed?" as if she were an object. As a white man who had married a black woman and adopted a black child, Loren truly felt that color did not matter. He couldn't understand the preoccupation with "what" Hydeia was.

By the time I returned to Loren, he was red in the face and talking loudly. He angrily described the couples picking up Hydeia and examining her as if she were a puppy at the pound. By the time the third couple inquired about Hydeia's racial background, Loren just about lost it. "What difference does it make whether she's black or mixed?" he yelled. "She's a baby who needs a home! That should be good enough."

While understandable, Loren's behavior wasn't exactly appropriate for the setting. To us, Hydeia wasn't just any baby to be picked up and looked over. She was Hydeia. The details that concerned these people didn't matter to us. I knew it was pointless to try to calm Loren down, so I was relieved when he announced, a little too loudly, "This is like a dog show. We're leaving!"

As we got Hydeia strapped back into her baby carrier and covered up, Loren said, "Hell, we love her, so why not keep her ourselves?" This was not the outcome I had anticipated, but I was overjoyed. In a funny way, the adoption fair was a success: Hydeia went home with a family that really loved her. Best of all, we never had to say good-bye.

Hydeia was our daughter now, and Keisha finally got the

"real" baby sister she always wanted. We couldn't have been happier. As the months rolled by, however, the changes that we expected to see in her never occurred. Feeding Hydeia was a daily exercise in frustration. We never found the "right" formula. Ever so slowly, she began putting on a little weight, but she still broke into screaming fits over nothing. She would be smiling and cooing happily one minute, then screaming inconsolably the next. Loren often felt frustrated over his inability to comfort her. I would explain that some babies, especially drug babies, could be sensitive like this. Maybe because I had more experience with babies, I had no problem leaving her in her room to cry. "As long as she's been fed, her diaper is dry, and there's nothing else wrong," I would tell Loren, "she's okay." Hydeia would cry and cry and cry, and on more than one occasion Loren, an otherwise laid-back type, punched a hole in a door out of frustration. Though it was easier for me to put her down and walk away, I have to admit that there were times when I wondered how much longer this would go on and why we couldn't help her.

By this point, we had accepted that this was just how Hydeia was. I remember switching her to Lactaid milk, thinking lactose intolerance was the problem, but like everything else we had tried, it had no effect. Once she started eating solid food, we hoped that she might find something she really liked to eat. By this point, I felt so frustrated I didn't even care what it was. If there was a new flavor of baby food out, I'd buy one jar on the chance that this could be "it"—the magic food she would actually eat. More often than not, though, Hydeia wouldn't be interested. So you can imagine how excited I was the first time she finished a whole jar. I'll never forget what it was, either: applesauce with strawberries and pineapple.

"God, she likes this!" I told Loren, then sent him running up to the local Safeway for more. Of course, the next day when I touched the spoonful of applesauce to her lips, she wouldn't even open her mouth. And that's how it was—and would be—for many years to come.

The vomiting and the diarrhea never stopped, either, and despite all our efforts, she was well below average in terms of height and weight for her age. At six months, when most babies weigh between sixteen and eighteen pounds, she weighed just twelve, which would have been fine for a baby half her age. At three, she was still wearing toddler pull-up disposable diapers because even though she had the ability to be potty-trained, her stool was so watery she just couldn't hold it in. I remember Hydeia running into the house, crying, "Keisha made me poop in my pants!" When I asked how that happened, Hydeia said, "She made me laugh." Of course, Hydeia soon realized that other kids her age were not wearing diapers. We continued going to doctors, hoping to find a solution. But we never did, and we just coped with it.

Those first three years Hydeia was sick with one thing or another almost all the time. She caught any cold that came around and seemed to have a perpetual upper-respiratory infection. Her nose was constantly stuffed with thick mucus she couldn't even blow out. At four months she caught chicken pox, which is extremely rare in healthy babies, since they usually still retain some of their mother's immunity. Stranger yet, whereas most people who catch chicken pox develop a lifelong immunity and never have it again, Hydeia would have chicken pox several times again. With the first bout, the blisterlike pox became infected and her doctor assumed she had developed a common but painful case of impetigo. In fact, what she had was shingles, a skin condition that results from infection by the same virus that causes chicken pox, herpes zoster. Although children commonly contract chicken pox, shingles usually doesn't develop until years—usually decades—afterward. Shingles emerges when the herpes zoster virus attacks a nerve, resulting in a red, blistery rash that can be intensely itchy and may cause a burning sensation or pain. Hydeia could not stop scratching the blisters, so they would fill with fluid, then burst. They were particularly bad under her arms and across her back, and she still has deep scars from the sores.

Over time her constant upper-respiratory infections began invading her sinuses. Sinus cavities have a limited blood supply, so it can take a lot of antibiotic over a long period to knock out an infection. Hydeia had so many sinus infections it was practically a constant condition. Sometimes the stuff inside her nose was so thick she could hardly breathe. If I could suction some of it out, it was as if a dam had burst, and what came out was foul-smelling and green. With each infection, it seemed to get worse, and there were times when I would look at what came out of that little nose and wonder where it was coming from. It seemed impossible that all that junk could be inside that tiny head. Again, doctors were baffled, and no one had an answer.

Considering that and the fact that she didn't eat well, it wasn't all that surprising that she reacted poorly to routine immunizations. After four kids, I thought I had seen just about everything, and I knew that some kids do have a little reaction—fussiness, a low-grade fever, maybe a rash—after receiving a vaccine. However, nothing prepared me for the way Hydeia responded. Within hours of the first shot, Hydeia was running a high fever and very sick. When I described her symptoms and my concerns to her doctor, he would say that some kids have an extreme response, it was nothing to worry about. But I did worry, and after the second immunization, I stopped taking her for them. I understood that by not vaccinating her, she was at risk for several potentially serious childhood illnesses. However, it was hard for me to imagine anything making her sicker than this. We, along with her pediatrician, had come to accept that all of this resulted from the lack of prenatal care and exposure to drugs in the womb.

Despite her poor health, Hydeia was a bright, alert, and curious child with a mind of her own and a real cute personality. She loved to sing and would make up songs off the top of her head about anything and everything. When she was ready to perform, she let you know. If we were all watching television, she would come in, turn off the television, do her thing, and then turn the television back on again. Like any little girl, she liked to dance and play dress-up. I can still picture her sauntering around the house in some elaborate outfit she had thrown together, complete with feather boa.

It was also nice to see the relationship that developed between Hydeia and each of my other children, especially Keisha. Being the older sister after so many years of being "the baby" appealed to Keisha, and she was very protective of her little sister. Except for the hours when Keisha was at school, the two of them did almost everything together. They ate together, played together, bathed together, slept together.

I had continued working, so at about six months of age, Hydeia began going to day care in a nursery school. She loved being around other kids and was very social, even as a baby. The staff didn't have a problem with the fact that she seemed to have a constant cold or, later, that she was still wearing diapers past the point when most other kids had been trained. They cared about Hydeia; she was in good hands. It was a happy, bright place, and she looked forward to going.

For those first three years we were living our lives—just a normal American family. Sure, Hydeia had more than her share of medical problems, but we never thought of her as "sick." Except for being perennially small for her age, Hydeia was developmentally on track. She walked, talked, and did all the things kids do when she was supposed to do them. Unlike many other drug-exposed babies, she didn't seem to have any behavioral or cognitive problems. Looking back, it's hard to say exactly what I thought about the illnesses and her other problems. We would cope with each challenge as it arose. We hoped she eventually

would outgrow her fussy eating habits and the chronic infections. Like most mothers, I listened to the doctor, and the expla-
nations I heard made sense. Hydeia was a kid who, from the
physical standpoint, just didn't get the best start in life. After all,
what other explanation could there be?

It was 1988 when the landscape of our lives changed forever. As
you will see, there have been a handful of blinding moments
when the reality of what lay ahead for Hydeia and all of us
flashed upon us. In truth, those moments marked only awareness. The forces that would shape Hydeia's life and our family's
actually had been at work months, maybe even years, before she
was born.

The first such moment came New Year's Day, though its significance would not be clear until sometime later. Loren and I
weren't really into drinking, so we went down to the strip in Las
Vegas, where New Year's Eve was always festive, with live music
and entertainment. The next day we stayed home and relaxed.
We sat down to dinner and switched on the six o'clock news.
There was a special report about "the first" baby born in Las
Vegas who was infected with HIV—though the reporter mis-
stated that the child "had AIDS." What made this newsworthy
was that this little boy was an otherwise healthy baby that the
hospital had no reason to keep. His mother had abandoned him,
and the hospital fully expected Child Haven to take him until a
suitable placement could be found. But Child Haven refused to
take in a child with HIV. I remember turning to Loren and saying, "That's ridiculous. They've probably had other babies with
HIV or AIDS. They just didn't know it."

As it turns out, I was more right on that point than I knew.
However, by no means was I what you would call educated on
the subject of HIV and AIDS. Like most Americans at that time,
I had heard about AIDS, but I can't say that I'd gone out of my

way to educate myself on the topic. AIDS had been in the news since 1982, when the term "acquired immune deficiency syndrome" was first coined. In the first few years after that, it seemed like a strange, rare disease that affected gay men, IV drug users, people who were sexually promiscuous, and a handful of people who had received HIV-infected blood or blood products. Since no one in our family fit into any of those categories, it wasn't something I believed I had much reason to think about.

As I would later learn, I was wrong about this, too. By late 1986 the number of AIDS cases diagnosed in the United States—42,255—had increased a hundredfold from 1981, when just 422 were known. From the beginning of 1987 until the end, the number of AIDS cases would jump from 42,255 to 71,176. Of those diagnosed from the beginning of the epidemic, more than 41,000 would be dead. And although a baby being born with HIV seemed rare enough to be newsworthy, there really was nothing new about it; as early as 1981 Dr. James Oleske at Newark Children's Hospital in New Jersey had tried to alert the government and his colleagues to a pattern he had observed in babies born to mothers who were drug addicts or prostitutes and/or who suffered from severely compromised immune systems. He was convinced that these babies had AIDS and, further, that he had seen his first case of pediatric AIDS as early as 1976. But hardly anyone believed him. In the history of AIDS, there were many stories like Dr. Oleske's, of doctors and other health professionals sounding an alarm the government inexplicably chose not to heed. Three years would elapse between the realization that HIV is a blood-borne agent and the testing of the blood supply. The United States would be six years into the epidemic before President Ronald Reagan ever publicly uttered the word *AIDS*. By the end of 1987, 737 children would be diagnosed with full-blown AIDS. Most of them contracted the virus from their mothers, yet at that time no one could tell you exactly how that might have occurred or how it could have been prevented.

That New Year's Day, however, I knew none of this. I did wonder what would become of this baby boy no one wanted. Who would open their home to a child with HIV? If I searched my own heart then, I knew that I wouldn't have. Remember, this was at a time when nearly half of all Americans believed you could contract the virus from a toilet seat. I remember thinking how sad it was but never talking to anyone about it. It was just an item on the news.

One late afternoon the following April, Marti, Hydeia's caseworker, phoned me at home. Marti was also on the board of MAMA, so we knew each other pretty well. I guess that's why it annoyed me when the first thing she said was, "Are you sitting down?"

Granted, I am not always the most patient person in the world, and I know that when someone asks if you're sitting down, they're probably getting ready to drop a bomb. "Marti, what do you mean, am I sitting down?"

"Well, I need to talk with you," she replied.

"Well, then, *talk* to me!" I snapped.

"Do you remember hearing about that little baby that was born on New Year's Day?" she asked.

"The baby with AIDS?" I answered, thinking to myself, *Why is she asking me this?*

"Yeah."

"Yeah, I remember."

"Well, the woman who gave birth to that boy is Hydeia's birth mother."

It took a few seconds for the possible implications of that fact to sink in. "I think you should probably get Hydeia tested, because we don't know if she could have been infected then."

"Okay," was all I said. I hung up the phone feeling like someone had just slapped me across the face. Then I started thinking about everything that had happened. I didn't know a lot about HIV and AIDS, but I did know that people who had it were sick all the time, and that certainly fit Hydeia. I thought about the constant respiratory infections, the bizarre outbreaks of chicken pox and shingles, and the diarrhea. Her reaction to immunizations, her eating problems, and her inability to gain weight—all the mysteries we attributed to her being a drug baby suddenly made more sense. The more I thought about it, the less I could deny the possibility that Hydeia might have AIDS.

I called Loren, who was a glazier and had a flexible schedule. He came right home. By then I was frantic, thinking about all the ways we might have been exposed to the virus as well. None of us had ever taken any special precautions with Hydeia. We ate off the same dishes, drank out of the same glasses. Like most families, we didn't think twice about taking a bite out of someone else's cookie or pizza. And Hydeia was just a kid. She had taken baths with Keisha and piddled in the water accidentally more than once, I was sure. She had gone through that toddler phase of biting her sister. I even recalled a couple of times when the phone rang right after I got her out of a bath and she had piddled on my lap. I had cleaned up her diapers, her vomit, her blood, and the green stuff that kept coming out of her nose. I never wore gloves. *What if . . .* I had to stop myself. The possibility that Hydeia might be infected was almost too terrible to imagine. I tried not to think about the rest of us, but my mind kept racing.

Fortunately, Loren was able to keep it together. "Let's just not ponder it," he said. "Make the appointment to have her tested, and we'll see."

I tried to push my concerns from my mind. After all, it was entirely possible that Hydeia's mother was not HIV-positive when Hydeia was born. I called Dr. G. immediately and made an appointment for the next day.

When we showed up for the appointment, Dr. G.'s receptionist greeted us and said, "Oh, he's waiting for you. Go in the back office." I sat down with Hydeia, and a few minutes later the doctor came in wearing a gown, hat, goggles, booties, and gloves. I couldn't believe my eyes.

"What does this test involve?" I asked.

"I have to take her blood," he replied.

"Take her blood?" I was incredulous; he was outfitted as if he was ready to perform open-heart surgery—in space. "Why have you got on all that stuff?"

He explained that it was possible to catch HIV and that he was taking precautions. Hydeia started screaming the minute he entered the room. He must have looked like a monster to her. I don't think she even knew who the heck he was.

After he drew her blood, he turned to me and said, "Now, you know we all have to start taking precautions."

I understood that he was saying what he was supposed to say, but the whole situation made me angry. "Well, you've been treating Hydeia since she was six weeks old. If it's that easy to catch, you've probably already got it and so do I." From the look on his face, it was clear he didn't exactly appreciate that, but it was the truth. He told me the results would take somewhere between four and five weeks, because her blood had to be sent to California. Hydeia was still crying, so I packed her up and we left.

Back at home, I told Loren what had happened. I couldn't believe how upset I was. "We'll just wait," he said. "We'll just wait."

From that moment and through the weeks before the test results came in, I moved through my life in a haze. No one had yet suggested that any of the rest of us be tested, but I knew that if Hydeia's test was positive, that would be the next step. Now, I know most people would have panicked and run straight to the drugstore for cases of rubber gloves, gowns, masks, and what-have-you before they changed another diaper or even wiped her nose, but I didn't. I'm not saying I wasn't afraid that she might have HIV and that some or all of the rest of us might, too. I was damn scared, more scared than I've ever been in my life. Yet from the little I did know about the virus, it didn't seem like something you would pick up from casual contact. If, however, the everyday exposure to diapers, snot, vomit, and even bites could transmit the virus, then we were all probably infected anyway, so what difference would it make? It seemed cruel to do anything that would make Hydeia feel different about herself or give her the impression that we felt different toward her. What would go through her mind when suddenly Mommy wouldn't help her out of her messy pull-ups without first putting on gloves, or kiss her boo-boos or let her share a bath with Keisha? I guess if you're really that afraid of the virus, those aren't even considerations. For me, though, they were big ones. I wasn't about to do anything that would make my child feel like something was wrong with her or that we were afraid of her.

I truly believed that. And then suddenly I'd start thinking about how I had little cuts on my hands from running the presses that imprinted type on plastic containers, like yogurt cups. (I'd quit social work and sort of lost myself in a supervisory position at a printing plant, which I really enjoyed.) If anyone had contracted the virus, it would have been me. Then the next minute I'd manage to get it all under control. At least for a while. Loren and I realized that it wasn't good for either of us or for the kids to let our emotions run away with us. There were moments when we were hysterical, but until Hydeia's results came in, we really didn't know what we were dealing with. In fact, we wouldn't really know until the rest of us were tested, and those results would take another five or six weeks. Even that would not necessarily be the final verdict, since we would be tested every six months or so for the next year and a half. But I couldn't even think about *that*.

Then the phone call came. Dr. G. said only that he had the test results and asked me to bring Hydeia in.

"What are the results?" I asked, my heart pounding.

"I can't tell you over the phone," he said. Of course, I knew what that meant, but I still had to know for sure. Loren couldn't come, so I took Hydeia to Dr. G.'s office. Probably without meaning to do it or even realizing it, the doctor made it clear that there was now something different about Hydeia and about me. He was sitting behind his desk acting strangely when we walked in. One thing I'd always liked about him was his warmth. He never saw me or Loren in the three years Hydeia had been his patient without shaking my hand or touching my arm and asking, "How you doin'?" Not today. His manner was formal and reserved.

"The test is positive," he said, looking straight at me. "She has AIDS."

"What does that mean?" I asked. As much as I had prepared myself to expect this, there was no way to absorb the shock of actually hearing the words.

He explained that there was no cure for AIDS. There was one medication that targeted the virus itself, but it was relatively new and not available to children. (Later I realized he was referring to AZT.) He didn't know what to tell me.

Within a few days the county health department contacted us. Dr. G. had had to inform the county of Hydeia's diagnosis. Loren and I went together. No one bothered to offer hope, because at that time there was none. Instead, at one point, a caseworker who knew us well asked, "Do you want to keep her?"

"What do you mean, do I want to keep her?" I asked, incredulous. "She's mine." The thought of giving her back or not wanting to continue being her parents never crossed our minds. Later it occurred to me that if Hydeia had been permanently disabled after getting hit by a car or had developed a different kind of terminal disease, like cancer, that question would never be asked. Yet because it was AIDS, that made it "different." But how? AIDS was an infection, just like any other infection.

Although by the time Hydeia was diagnosed the Centers for Disease Control had reported more than seven hundred children with AIDS, there was only one study of pediatric AIDS going on, and it had begun only the year before. The medical establishment was just waking up to the fact that children could even contract HIV and develop AIDS. The information Hydeia's doctors needed to help her simply did not exist.

All they could tell us was what to expect, and that was based on the only thing they knew: what had happened to other children with AIDS. They died. The doctor there also told us that there were no medications available for children at that time. Less than a year before, the Food and Drug Administration had approved AZT (zidovudine, or Retrovir), the first drug that demonstrated an ability to attack the virus itself. Unfortunately, it had produced severe side effects in some adults and had not been approved for use by children.

All we could do was wait for the inevitable infections and complications to arise, then try to treat them. Of course, nothing we would do to treat a sinus infection or a bout of chicken pox would have any impact on the virus itself. It would continue invading her immune cells, producing copies of itself, which, in turn, would hijack other immune cells until she finally encountered the one infection her body could not defeat. Hydeia probably would not live to see five. Given the fate of most other children born with the virus, many doctors would tell me in the coming years, it was amazing she had lived until then. Hydeia was a few months short of four that day. I remember thinking, *Her life is more than three quarters over.*

They have yet to invent the words for what I felt that day. My heart filled with sadness and hopelessness. I wanted to scream. At whom or what, I didn't know. Everything about the situation overwhelmed me. Hydeia was going to die. Over the past few weeks, I'd managed to stop myself from wondering what else the future held for us, which of the rest of us might also be infected, and what that might mean. That, as Loren would say, we would deal with after we knew about Hydeia. Now that they were taking blood from Loren, Keisha, and me for testing, I couldn't ignore the possibility that any or all of us might be infected, too. My fears came in the form of variations on the same question: "What if?" What if Loren, or I, or Keisha also had the virus? What if it was just me or just Loren or me and Loren? What if Keisha was orphaned, or if Loren and I fell sick or died before Hydeia or Keisha? What if we were going to lose both of our daughters? What if we were all dying? The prospect of loving someone, or being someone, destined to die of a disease for which there was neither hope nor treatment darkened my soul.

If you had asked me a month or two before, I could have told you exactly what I'd be doing five, ten, twenty years later. We had it all planned out. Suddenly, life itself was a question mark. As quickly and as clearly as if someone had flipped a switch, despair replaced light. Watching the lab tech fill vial after vial with my blood, I was certain beyond doubt that my test would also be positive. When the test results showed that no one else had contracted the virus, we were all relieved. At the same time, I was angry and impatient. I remember thinking of the doctors predicting doom. *They don't even know what they're talking about.* To be fair, that was not exactly true. At the time, whoever we spoke with knew a lot more about HIV and AIDS than I did. However, knowing "a lot" about it then was not the same as knowing enough. I couldn't look at these past nearly four years—with Hydeia's infections, the Las Vegas medical authorities believing her brother was their first "AIDS baby," or anything doctors had said or done since we decided to test Hydeia—and not wonder, *How much else don't they know?*

These thoughts were frightening yet strangely empowering. Maybe the hopelessness wasn't the whole story. Maybe somewhere someone else knew more about how to treat children like Hydeia. At this point, you might imagine a mother like me taking control, turning the world upside down to get my daughter what she needed. But that didn't happen. There was no Internet like what we have today, no books, no organizations devoted to pediatric AIDS. (HIV and AIDS attack adults and children in very different ways.) All the anger, rage, and determination burning inside me withered before the "fact" that Hydeia was going to die. Not possibly, not probably, but definitely.

I had no problem letting most people know that she had HIV. Though there were so many stories in the news about discrimination and even acts of violence against people with AIDS, it seemed to me that who knew what and what they thought about it were the least of my problems. To be honest, I really didn't care.

What I did care about was Hydeia. Throughout that first year and for some time afterward, I couldn't talk about her without breaking down. In fact, about a year would pass between the time Hydeia was diagnosed and when I told my three older kids, Kendall, Pepe, and Kim. This might seem inconsistent with my feelings about disclosure, but I saw it as a mother. As distraught as I felt, for my children I still needed to be in control, to deliver the news in a moment when I could say—and believe—that there was hope. When I told them, I wanted to have the same calm, stoic manner my mother always did. I wanted them to take away from the news some sense of hope, or at least not the hopelessness I was feeling then. Later, when I did tell them, they each rose to the occasion. For example, Kendall requested and was granted a transfer so he could complete his tour of duty closer to home. My other children always were there to pitch in whenever we needed them. By then several of my siblings were living nearby, as well as my mother. Ours was not an overtly emotional family, and my mother, as always, was there for me and our family in her own quiet way. I was trying so hard to keep it together, to be the rock for my children the way she had always been for me and my siblings, but I was failing.

Before that calm descended upon me, I was a mess. Hydeia and Keisha would run by playing, and all I could think was, *She's going to die.* Naturally, whoever I told about her would ask, "So what are they going to do?" and every time I answered, "They aren't going to do anything! She's going to die!" Considering that this was, we were told, probably her last year with us, my memories of the time are not what you might expect. What might have been her last birthday the following June, her last Christmas, her last Easter—all the special moments—passed in a blur. I could become emotionally overwhelmed just hearing Hydeia laugh. In my mind, I actually pictured her as a little windup toy with a key in her back. Every second she was "ticking," like a time bomb. We were in a holding pattern, paralyzed, just waiting for the inevitable, waiting for her to die. In the meantime, life went on. I continued working at the printing plant, where the steady, rhythmic sounds of the press in operation and the regularity of the routine were a welcome contrast to my real life at home.

When it came to telling the people who worked at Hydeia's nursery school about the diagnosis, I never hesitated. While I wasn't about to "suit up" in protective gear every time I went near my daughter, I realized that anyone caring for her needed to know. Most important, though, we all needed to be vigilant on behalf of the person most at risk, and that was Hydeia. Nursery schools are hotbeds of childhood infections, any one of which could prove fatal to Hydeia. I needed to know if any of the other kids were sick or had just been vaccinated, because some live-virus vaccines, such as one against polio, can infect others with compromised immunity. I truly believed that knowing that no one else in our family was infected, despite never having taken precautionary measures, would ease some of the staff's worries. After all, I reasoned, they had been caring for her all this time without the knowledge. Now that they knew and knew what to do, it should be fine. After all, I was a living, walking, talking example of how difficult it was to contract HIV through routine caregiving. I thought I had my case all sewn up. I was wrong.

When I dropped Hydeia off one morning, I talked with one of the caregivers. I told her that Hydeia had tested positive for HIV, that she had had it all of her life, and that no one else in our family had gotten it, despite our exposure to her blood and other bodily fluids. I told the woman that I needed to know if any of the children got sick, particularly with chicken pox or whooping cough. She seemed to be taking the news all right. At one point, she said simply, "Oh, I'm so sorry."

About two hours later I got a call at work asking me to come to the nursery school. There the director told me that the school was not equipped to take care of Hydeia. It made no sense to me, because Hydeia was exactly the same that day as she had been the day before. The only difference was that now they knew she had HIV. The director dealt with me by not acknowledging anything I said and simply reiterating that they did not have the "facilities" to handle a child like Hydeia. It was a ridiculous position to take, especially considering that all they needed in the way of "facilities" was some soap, water, latex gloves, and bleach. I'd worked in social services long enough and knew the law well enough to understand that she was not about to expose the nursery school to a lawsuit by suggesting that they didn't want Hydeia.

Looking back, I shouldn't have been surprised, but I was. I got Hydeia's things together and left with her in my arms. The next day, I called the county health department to tell them what had happened. Instead of sharing my outrage, their position was that I probably shouldn't have said anything and that in the future I shouldn't, either. They suggested that if I wanted to pursue it, however, I could sue the nursery school. As upset as I was, I didn't want to do that. Yes, maybe the nursery school could be coerced legally into accepting her. But what would that mean for Hydeia if she went back? They didn't want her in the first place, so there was no way that a judge or any other authority telling them they had to take her would change that. I pictured her back in the nursery school but being treated differently—isolated, and feared. I refused to do that to her. Instead, I found someone to care for her at home. I felt fortunate to find a woman who was familiar with HIV and AIDS because someone in her own family was then coping with it. She would know the signs and symptoms to look for, I thought. Hydeia would be safe.

People at the county health department told me about Dr. K., a pediatric pulmonary specialist who was the only doctor in our area then treating children with AIDS. Dr. K. had a warm, caring manner, and I liked him immediately. We talked as he examined Hydeia, and at one point he said, "I'm surprised she's in as good shape as she is." He asked if I had any questions or concerns, and I mentioned the relentless sinus infections. Those were typical for kids with HIV and AIDS, he told me, and he reiterated that we would just fight each infection as it arose. Though Dr. K. had far more experience with pediatric AIDS than any doctor we'd worked with so far, his prognosis echoed everyone else's.

In the course of running a battery of tests, Dr. K. had taken X rays of Hydeia's lungs. We were trying to account for her low-grade fever and her constant lack of stamina. As he pointed out to me, there were spots on her lungs caused by lymphoid interstitial pneumonia (LIP), the result of a direct attack of the HIV on the lungs. In these spots the normally soft, elastic lung tissue had been replaced by hard, nodulelike tissue that did not expand when she breathed. As a result, Hydeia was not always getting as much oxygen as she needed; this would become more dramatically apparent when we started flying regularly. The LIP also made it more likely that infection could settle into her lungs, and pneumonia of any kind was and still is a leading AIDS-related cause of death. Most children with AIDS develop LIP, and there is no cure.

Around that time I also learned that in addition to Hydeia and her half brother Michael, there were three other children in Las Vegas who had been diagnosed. More than once I was given the phone numbers of two other adoptive mothers—Diana Dowling, who had adopted Michael, and Cindy Small, who, with her husband, Larry, had adopted a boy named Tyler—and encouraged to contact them. A woman named Mary Anne at the county health department told me that she had formed a support group where Diana, Cindy, and the mothers of Anna Lee and Tiffany, the two other children, got together. Having run support groups of one kind or another most of my adult life, I understood the purpose they served. They were fine for other people, I felt, but not for me. The only thing I could envision was a group of us sitting in a circle crying about our kids being sick and dying. No thank you. I was doing that well enough on my own. It was not something I could picture myself doing among a group of strangers. Of course, taking Hydeia to Dr. K.'s, I did run into these mothers. One day Cindy, who was baby-sitting Michael for Diana, approached me.

"Oh, this must be Hydeia," she said.

"Yes," I replied.

"This is Mikey," she said, smiling. I looked at the little boy who was either Hydeia's brother or half brother. He, too, seemed small for his age.

"Oh," I answered. I admit, I was not very friendly then. Despite that, Cindy kept making overtures, inviting me to bring Hydeia over for play dates and offering to baby-sit her. Many times she said, "If you ever need my help, or just want to talk, give me a ring."

"Sure," I'd say, while thinking, *How are you going to support me? What do you know that they don't know?* I would be offered refuge many times before I finally accepted.

"Treatment" for Hydeia then consisted of managing whatever infections or problems cropped up and giving her a transfusion of gamma globulin every three weeks. Occurring naturally in the blood, gamma globulin is proteins that work as antibodies and fight off infection. The commercial preparation that Hydeia received was made from blood and contained antibodies that provided a limited, "passive" immunity to a wide range of infectious agents. It did not "boost" or improve her own immune system, which the HIV was decimating. Instead, it was more like temporarily borrowing an outside immune system to help do some of the work.

When I learned that the gamma was transfused over three or four hours, I knew I could never stand to accompany Hydeia for the treatments. Regular doctor's appointments I could handle. But just picturing that little thing with a needle stuck in her arm was more than I could handle. Loren took her to her first treatment, and after they got her hooked up, he called. The first thing I asked was, "Is she crying?"

"Well, she was crying, but now she's okay," he assured me. "She wants to talk to you."

"Okay." A few seconds later I heard Hydeia's voice.

"Mommy, why did you let them stick me?" she wailed into the phone before bursting into tears.

I fought to hold back my tears and remain calm as I explained, "You have to take this medicine, Hydeia. You'll be okay, and I'll see you when you get home. Now, let me talk to Daddy."

I started crying, and when Loren came back on the line, he was crying, too. "I can't do this," I said, sobbing. "I can't."

"We're going to get through this," he said. "We'll get through it."

For the first year Loren took care of everything that had to do with medicine and treatments. Because gamma is extraordinarily expensive—over two thousand dollars an infusion—and does not keep more than a few hours after it's been mixed, once you made an appointment, you were stuck with it. Though we had good health insurance, we were still responsible for 20 percent of the cost of each infusion (about four hundred dollars) once it was mixed, whether Hydeia got it or not. And of course, there was the more important matter of keeping up the gamma to protect her.

Usually Loren called the hospital to mix the gamma globulin about four hours before he would take Hydeia in. One day, about two hours before her appointment, he had an emergency at work he couldn't get out of. Knowing how upset I would be, he came home to tell me, "You're going to have to take Hydeia to get her meds."

"Oh, God," I said. Remembering Hydeia crying over the phone during that first infusion, what little bit of toughening up I'd done since she had been diagnosed fell away. "I don't know if I can do it. She's going to be crying, I'll be crying."

"No, no, Pat. She doesn't cry anymore," he assured me. "She's real good. She just sits there and gets the needle, and it's fine. You can do it, because she can do it."

"Okay," I said, though deep in my heart I feared I would lose it. No sooner had we parked the car than it became clear that Hydeia knew what she was doing. I'd never been there before, but she knew exactly where to go, the AIDS ward, and Keisha and I followed. When she saw her nurse, she happily said, "Hi, Claude."

"Who's this?" he asked her, smiling at me and Keisha.

"This is my mommy and this is my sister."

He greeted us, and without any prompting, Hydeia took off her jacket, jumped up on the table, took off her shirt, stuck out her arm, and was ready to go. When Claude inserted the needle, Hydeia didn't flinch or make a sound. I couldn't believe it. Here I was, waiting for the tears—hers or mine, I wasn't sure—but nothing. Then, after five minutes, Hydeia said to Claude in a way that let you know she knew what she was talking about, "This is a bad vein. It hurts. You need to get another one."

"Okay," he said. He gently removed the needle.

"Here," she said, pointing to another vein. "Put it here."

I watched in amazement at how cool and relaxed she was. My four-year-old daughter had come further in accepting and dealing with her disease than I had. Something inside me had to change.

TWO

The next day I called the health department and asked for all the information they had on AIDS. I needed to learn everything, to make up for lost time before time ran out. It was early 1989, and I was finally looking ahead and allowing myself to hope. She would be starting kindergarten that fall, probably the first child in the Las Vegas public school system known to have HIV. I was determined that this would not be a replay of what had happened in nursery school. For the first time, I stopped focusing on my grief and started facing reality. Hydeia was still here. We had a mission, but we had no allies. For the first time, I admitted to myself that I needed help.

Not long after that trip to the hospital with Hydeia, I was sitting with Cindy and Tyler, Diana and Mikey, and Tiffany and her grandmother. As AIDS took away parents, sometimes before their infected children, you saw a lot of children being cared for by grandparents. By that time, a fifth child, Anna Lee, had died. Tiffany, who was about two, was so impaired by the virus that she still had not learned to walk. Over the years, I would meet many children like her, who were physically and developmentally far behind their chronological age.

I often wonder if the devil was watching me when I was bad. If the devil was watching me, I know GOD would fight the devil and win.

I often wonder if my first mommy was nice. I think she was taking drugs. I don't think I would like her if I met her now because she took drugs and made me have the virus.

I often wonder what Heaven is like. I think there is angels all over, baby angels and grown up angels. I think I will be happy in Heaven.

Hydeia
Age six

Of course, I already knew Cindy from Dr. K.'s office, and I knew Diana was Hydeia's half brother Mikey's adoptive mother. Though Cindy, Diana, and I had very different personalities, we naturally banded together, sort of like the Three Musketeers. While Hydeia, Tyler, and Mikey all became great friends, Cindy, Diana, and I helped one another however we could, becoming our own informal support network. We baby-sat, we shared information, we grew close. We talked together, fought together, and sometimes cried together. After trying to handle this myself, alone (except for Loren), I welcomed having two good people outside my family I could count on. They, more than anyone, really understood what I was going through. They listened and, most important, allowed me to say how I really felt about things without the well-intended but annoying platitudes other people offered. Regardless of the faces we presented to the world, we were all uncertain and terrified of what lay ahead. We could talk to one another about what was going on with the kids medically without having to stop every two minutes to translate the foreign language of meds, techniques, tests, diseases, and conditions.

Cindy stayed at home with her children and watched Mikey. Diana, like me, was a working mom who saw the urgent need for quality day care for our kids. We approached a local AIDS organization in the hope that we could establish a resource for families of children with HIV and AIDS under its umbrella. As I quickly learned, however, people who were ignorant and unaffected by AIDS were not the only ones who viewed the disease in political rather than medical terms. Perhaps I was naïve to think that Hydeia's being asked to leave nursery school because of her HIV status was as outrageous and wrong as an adult's being refused work, housing, or insurance because of his. Unfortunately, this group's leadership (primarily gay and white) just was not interested in our problems.

Sure, we were disappointed; it was a setback but not a total loss. For one thing, their response forced us to see that if there was anything that we thought our kids needed, we would have to find it or create it ourselves. While that might sound depressing, that realization gave us the drive and focus that would result in some positive changes, not only for our children but for many others as well. We began looking into creating our own place for children with HIV and AIDS and their siblings. And we got one other thing out of our visit with the AIDS organization: Someone there casually mentioned an upcoming AIDS conference in Los Angeles we might be interested in attending.

It was now spring 1989, about a year after Hydeia's diagnosis. While "officially" Hydeia had not developed the symptoms and illnesses indicating that her infection had crossed over from HIV to full-blown AIDS, there was no denying the direction she was headed. At times it seemed as if everything that could go wrong did. Her red-blood-cell count could not be maintained, so she had to have transfusions. If she crossed paths with anyone who had a routine strep throat, the strep would invade her blood. Before long, no one who visited our home got through the front door without a full medical background "check." Later, I would go with Hydeia to Los Angeles once every month, so Dr. Joseph A. Church, a specialist in pediatric AIDS, could monitor her at Children's Hospital. Working in conjunction with Dr. K., Dr. Church ran the tests that tracked her T-cell count and other critical developments. (The "helper," or CD4, T cells are active lymphocytes, the immune cells that identify and attack infectious agents. The lower your T-cell count, the more susceptible you are to infection.)

Although Hydeia had grown to be a bright, happy, friendly, and otherwise normal kid, we still couldn't get a handle on some of her chronic problems. When, if, how, what, and how much she ate remained an ongoing obsession for all of us. Before we knew she had HIV, improving her nutritional status and getting some weight on her was a concern. Now that we knew what she was up against, it felt like a war.

Every day I'd come home from work and ask Hydeia's baby-sitter, "Well, did she eat?"

Every day the answer was the same: "Well, first she said she wanted eggs, and then when I got the eggs done, she didn't want them anymore, she wanted noodles. . . ." Lined up on the kitchen counter like a kiddie buffet would be a dish of noodles next to a bowl of oatmeal next to a plate of scrambled eggs—all now cold, none of them touched. I had left the sitter with explicit instructions to make Hydeia whatever she wanted, whenever she wanted it. I later learned that many people with HIV and AIDS become sensitive to the smell of food, sometimes to the point where it makes them lose their appetite. I was able to get Hydeia to drink a little bit of Ensure, the nutritional-supplement drink, but she would throw that up once she had had enough. Whatever she would eat, we would do whatever we had to to get it for her. If that meant a late-night run to McDonald's for Chicken McNuggets, that's what we did.

Our desperation for Hydeia to eat anything created problems for Keisha, whose first word upon tasting an avocado as a baby was simply "Delicious!" Keisha, who was a little heavy for her age, was Hydeia's polar opposite. Whereas Hydeia wouldn't eat anything, there didn't seem to be anything Keisha wouldn't eat. I know it seemed unfair to Keisha that we were encouraging Hydeia to eat as much of anything that she would, while we were trying to teach Keisha to eat less. With this, as with many issues in the years to come, I would feel that Hydeia's needs often and necessarily overshadowed Keisha's.

Loren, who got home from work before I did, would try to coax Hydeia into eating, but she wouldn't even pick up her spoon. If he got her to take a bite of something, she would chew and chew and chew without swallowing. Finally, he would give up and wait for me to feed her. Not that I could do much better, but it was difficult for him. Realizing how little control we had over something so basic, so simple, was frightening.

Throughout that spring, we continued battling the sinus infections, one after another, as we always had. Although they seemed to be getting a little worse—the mucus seemed thicker and was often bloody—Hydeia didn't appear ill. As I would soon learn, that was one of the virus's deadlier traps.

I came home from work one afternoon to an empty house. I was surprised the sitter had the girls out, because it was one of those incredibly hot—maybe as high as 110 degrees—Las Vegas days. *They must be out playing,* I thought. That gave me some time to myself, to shower and relax a little before starting dinner. I was sitting on the couch when Keisha suddenly burst through the door, followed by the sitter, who was carrying Hydeia in her arms. I took one look at my baby and knew something was terribly wrong. Hydeia looked like some force had just flung her onto her back and into the sitter's arms. Her head was hanging as if she was passed out or dead, and her arms and legs were as limp as a rag doll's. Oddly, though, the sitter seemed unconcerned.

"This is awful late for her to be sleeping," I said warily.

"She took a late nap," the sitter explained. "But she's been sleeping on and off all day."

"Bring her here," I said. As the sitter gently placed Hydeia in my lap, I couldn't believe how hot she was. "Keisha! Run and get me the new digital thermometer!"

Touching Hydeia's forehead, and especially around her face, under her chin, I could tell this was not a regular fever. I turned the thermometer on and slipped it under Hydeia's arm, so as to not awaken her. I had never used a digital thermometer before, so when the numbers on the little readout screen kept flying past the familiar 102, 103, on to 105.8 without beeping and stopping, I thought, *This is crazy. This thing must be broken.* I called Keisha over, turned the thermometer off, then on, and took her temperature: The readout stopped at 98.6. I cleared it again, placed it back under Hydeia's arm, and waited a few seconds for the beep: at 106 plus.

I still couldn't believe it. I tried it again on Keisha, then on myself. By then, to my shock, I realized that Hydeia was literally burning up alive. I jumped up off the couch and raced to the bathroom, where I placed her in a tub of lukewarm water and gave her a couple of Tylenol to start bringing down her fever. I called Dr. K., who told me to rush her to the hospital as soon as her temperature came down around 103. He didn't want me to move her now, because with such a high fever she was at risk for seizure or even brain death. He reminded me that because I had taken Hydeia's temperature under her arm, it was actually at least a half degree higher. He promised to meet us later at the pediatric ward, so we would not have to go through the hassle of admitting her through the emergency room.

While Hydeia was in the tub, I asked the sitter, "How long has she had this fever?"

"I didn't know she had a fever," the sitter replied.

I was incredulous. "She has AIDS! You have someone in your own family who has AIDS. Do you mean to tell me that if that person slept all day like this, you wouldn't take his temp or try to find out what was going on? I don't believe this. Just get out!"

I was furious and frightened as I kept taking Hydeia's temperature. Once it had fallen to 103, I rushed her to the car and flew to my mother's house, where I hastily dropped off Keisha before heading to the hospital. Dr. K. was there waiting and immediately got to work. Because Hydeia had HIV, his first, logical thought was that this must be pneumonia, but her chest was clear. "Have you noticed anything unusual about her?"

"Just her nose," I said. "But I've already told you about that." After years of struggling to loosen the congestion in her sinuses, they were still a mess. If she sneezed, a pussy, blood-streaked mucus that smelled horrible showered everything. Dr. K. listened, but the sinus problem had always been there. He believed something else was causing the fever, but after two days of testing revealed nothing, I suggested, "Maybe it's her sinuses."

"No, I don't think a sinus infection would do this," he insisted.

"Well, even if you don't think that's it, why don't you just humor me? Just culture her nose and see what you get," I said.

The cultures revealed streptococcus, staph, pseudomonas, and a host of other bacteria. Alarmed, Dr. K. called in an ear, nose, and throat specialist, Dr. R., who decided that Hydeia's sinuses had to be biopsied immediately.

When Dr. R. came out of surgery and approached Loren and me in the waiting room, she looked as if she didn't know what to say. "I have never seen a nasal canyon like Hydeia's before," she said. "If I didn't know any better, I would swear I was looking at someone who had been snorting cocaine for fifteen years." She went on to explain that there was no healthy pink tissue left in her nose, that everything was brown, gray, or discolored and decayed. She had scraped away whatever she could and was culturing that tissue for more pathogens or some cellular abnormality. But, she said ominously, "I'm afraid, Mrs. Broadbent, that Hydeia might have cancer or leprosy in her sinuses."

I couldn't say anything but "Okay." Cancer? Leprosy? As Loren and I walked upstairs to see Hydeia in recovery, I recalled how surprised Dr. K. had been when I showed him a napkin Hydeia had blown her nose into. It was full of mucus, pus, and what looked like pieces of dead skin. Shouldn't she be seeing an ear, nose, and throat specialist? I had asked more than once. He reassured me that all the kids with HIV and AIDS had bad sinuses and prescribed a heavy-duty oral antibiotic called Augmentin (amoxicillin and potassium clavulanate). Perhaps it wasn't fair of me to be angry with him. Even if he was the only doctor in Las Vegas who was treating pediatric AIDS, he could not have known everything. At that time, no one did. Who would ever have imagined what was going on inside Hydeia's head? Still, I was afraid for Hydeia, and getting angry quickly became one of my coping mechanisms.

When he said, "I think we need to discuss something," I just glared at him.

"I really don't feel like talking right now," I said, and started to walk away. I knew myself, and I knew that if I talked to him right then, I was likely to say something I would regret. After he insisted, I said, "I really feel that you are the reason she's in the shape she's in right now." I reviewed our history, the number of times I'd asked for a referral to a specialist, the smelly, disgusting globs of junk wrapped in tissue I'd shown him. "Now I'm here and she's down in the O.R. and Dr. R. thinks she's got cancer or leprosy in her damn sinuses!"

"Hold up, hold up," Dr. K. said. "You have to understand that I take care of many chronically ill children. Parents sometimes go overboard. They don't understand the science of medicine, and I have to go through and figure it out, and I have to read you—"

"Read me?" I snapped. "No. You do not ever read me. I will tell you when I have a problem, and I will tell you exactly what it is. When I tell you I've got a problem and I want it addressed, that's what I want done. I have never had a chronically ill child, and I may not know everything there is to know about AIDS. But from this day on, no one is ever going to tell me that anything I'm concerned about with Hydeia is 'normal' or 'what all the AIDS kids have.'" I walked away, fuming.

Despite my feelings then, I did not want to change doctors. All I wanted was for this doctor to start managing Hydeia's case the way I wanted it done. A few days after Hydeia left the hospital, we went to Dr. K. for a follow-up visit, and his first words when he saw me were, "Are we friends?"

"Yeah," I said. "We're friends. On the whole, you're a great doctor. Just don't ever try to read me."

"Okay," he said, smiling. "You've got my word. I understand your frustration and your anger, but I wish you would understand my situation."

"I do, Dr. K., but from this point on, all I want to hear from you is what we are going to do to help *her.* That's all." He understood.

That experience taught me a lot about dealing with doctors. I would never again sit back and quietly accept anything without questioning and, yes, even demanding. From then on, my attitude toward the medical profession was, "I don't care what happens to 'kids with AIDS.' It ain't happening to Hydeia. You do something." Firm, inflexible, demanding, difficult—I'm sure I've been called all those things and more, and if that's how some doctors and medical people saw it, that was fine with me. As long as they did their jobs, they could think what they liked. I wasn't out to win a popularity contest anyway. I was there to save my child.

When the biopsy results came back, Hydeia had neither cancer nor leprosy. However, this massive infection marked a downturn. The sinus infections continued, and then Hydeia's red-blood-cell count began dropping to dangerously low levels, necessitating blood transfusions. She remained on huge doses of antibiotics and received her gamma infusions. Still, she was beginning to lose ground. By then I had developed what you could call a sixth sense about Hydeia. A day or two before something happened, I would call the doctor and say I thought something was wrong. When asked exactly what I was seeing, I couldn't describe it. There was something about her eyes, and I know that it must have been confusing to hear me describe them as both dull and glassy, but they were, and sometimes a little reddish as well. She could be happily running around, looking just fine, but I would know that something was coming.

Later that summer Hydeia had her first bout of what is known as PCP, or pneumocystis carinii pneumonia. Before the rise of HIV, the pneumocystis carinii protozoa were rarely seen in human lungs; they thrived primarily in the lungs of guinea pigs and sewer rats. Pneumocystis is all around, but a healthy human immune system can destroy it easily. First noticed in 1942 as a cause of pneumonia in European wartime orphanages, PCP is one of several so-called opportunistic infections. It can take hold only when a person's compromised immune system presents an opportunity. The rise of HIV infection brought tens of thousands of cases of PCP. Before tests for HIV were developed, a bout of PCP was often the first—and for some, the fatal last—infection that heralded the presence of AIDS. For several years PCP would remain one of the most common causes of AIDS-related death. Medically speaking, having PCP was an "event" because it marked the dread "graduation" from HIV infection to full-blown AIDS. We had turned the corner onto a dead-end street.

In June 1989 Hydeia turned five, the age at which doctors had predicted she would probably die. The national pediatric AIDS conference we had heard about was coming up that fall, and although I had no idea what, if anything, I might find there to help her, a sense of urgency consumed me. Cindy was not working then and couldn't afford to go, so she took care of Mikey, and Diana and I made the trip. It was the first time I'd spent away from Hydeia since the diagnosis, but I knew that she was in good hands with Loren.

Diana and I flew to Los Angeles and checked in at the hotel where the conference was being held. The hotel was among the most luxurious in the world, and the prices were exorbitant, so Diana and I shared a room. The conference started the next day, and we were eager to get going. Of course, we went in knowing that it was a professional conference aimed primarily at doctors and health professionals, but once we saw the list of presentations, we knew we were in over our heads. Still, we were determined to come away with something, so we sat through a few talks about the status of current protocols, or drug trials, full of medical terminology we had no prayer of understanding. At one point I leaned over to Diana and said, "I think we each wasted our three hundred fifty dollars." That was just the cost of the room.

"No," she said, shaking her head firmly. "We're going to get something." Diana was a school principal, a no-nonsense type who could be assertive when it came to getting what she wanted. Where Cindy was typically soft-spoken and quiet, Diana and I were in many ways two of a kind. Before long, within the pediatric AIDS community, we were referred to as "Ebony and Ivory." While she listened to the speaker, I glanced through the program booklet listing all the presentations. My eye caught something about a pediatric longevity study, and the description mentioned a little girl who was considered the longest-surviving child with AIDS.

"Let's go to this session," I said to Diana, pointing to the page. "Let's see what's going on."

The two main speakers were Dr. James Oleske and Dr. Philip A. Pizzo. Although at the time we had no idea who they were, later I would look back and thank fate for this chance meeting with two pioneers of pediatric AIDS research and treatment. Dr. Oleske is credited with being the first doctor to identify HIV infection and AIDS in babies in 1981, and perhaps even as early as 1976. Dr. Philip Pizzo was the head of pediatrics at the National Cancer Institute (NCI). The NCI is part of the National Institutes of Health (NIH), which is made up of various institutes dedicated to different diseases. Located in Bethesda, Maryland, outside Washington, D.C., NIH has long been a world leader in research and treatment. Dr. Pizzo began his research on pediatric AIDS in 1986; before that, his focus was the treatment of infection in children with cancer. In 1986 he became the first to conduct pediatric clinical trials on AZT. Two years later Dr. Pizzo wrote the first article in *The New England Journal of Medicine* on antiviral therapy for children with AIDS, a landmark in the history of pediatric AIDS treatment. I was stunned to learn that in the summer of 1989, three years after the pediatric clinical trials had begun and a year after the journal article, no one treating Hydeia at home seemed to have heard of the trials. While NIH was not the only institution conducting clinical trials, it would remain at the forefront not only in trials but also in defining what constituted effective treatment of pediatric AIDS.

Diana and I listened as the doctors spoke about the case of an eleven-year-old girl who developed AIDS after receiving a blood transfusion during heart surgery at age nine. When I heard them say that she was not only the oldest child diagnosed with AIDS but the longest-surviving, I did some quick math. I tapped Diana and whispered, "Nine, ten, eleven. Diana, that's three years, tops. That's not damn longevity. That's the same track record Hydeia has."

The doctors described two new studies that they were starting in New Jersey and at NIH. In this next phase they were going to explore the possible pediatric use of CD4 (which I will explain later) and an oral form of ddI (didanosine), an antiviral like AZT. They began telling us about the study protocol, including the criteria a child must meet to be included. The child had to have had three opportunistic infections, and the T-cell count had to be under 200. There was no age limit. Diana and I looked at each other. Hydeia and Mikey (as well as Tyler and Tiffany) met the conditions. "Let's go up and talk to them when they're finished," I whispered.

After the presentation, droves of people surged toward the doctors, so Diana and I waited our turns. She started talking with Dr. Oleske, and I introduced myself to Dr. Pizzo. From the start, I was impressed by his gentle, soft-spoken manner. He looked younger than you would expect from his position, and from then on, I never spoke with him without feeling I had his full attention. He listened carefully as I described Hydeia's medical history: the sinus infections, PCP, shingles, LIP, pseudomonas, the T-cell count now hovering at just about 100—the point at which many people with AIDS succumb to opportunistic infections and die. I was very conscious of the fact that I described her as being "diagnosed at three and a half and now being over five years old." That age— five—had such significance to me. Though this was the first real chance anyone had offered my baby, I felt the weight of time pressing at my back and realized that this was her last chance, too. "Would she qualify?" I asked anxiously.

In his kind, gentle voice, he said, "Yes, I think she would qualify for the protocol." A wave of feelings—relief, joy, hope—washed over me, but I tried to stay focused as he described what to do next. "When you go home, have your doctor send NIH all of her medical records. We'll profile her, and if she fits, we'll contact you. You'll have to pay for the first trip to NIH, but we'll pay for your transportation home. Once she is on protocol, NIH will cover all the expenses related to her medical care there, including the medications, and contribute toward the cost of your food and lodging." After that, honestly, I wasn't even listening. I thanked Dr. Pizzo—many times, I'm sure—and went to find Diana.

She was as excited as I was and began telling me all about Dr. Oleske, how he had discovered AIDS in babies. I was nodding but not really listening. Diana had had much the same conversation with Dr. Oleske that I'd had with Dr. Pizzo, and Dr. Oleske was certain that Mikey would qualify, and so would Tyler. Words like *happy* and *elated* cannot begin to capture how we felt. Now we had a purpose and a focus.

Back in our room, we reviewed the conference brochures and discovered a couple of exhibits that looked interesting. We went to one that displayed medical equipment specially designed for children, which was a little strange to see. We saw special dolls that kids with AIDS could identify with, dolls that had Portocaths (catheters placed semipermanently into major veins to eliminate the need for constant needle sticks to draw blood or administer medication) and Hickmans (another type of intravenous catheter). One exhibit that drew our interest was for the Association for the Care of Children's Health. We began talking with two ACCH representatives, Ippy and Josie, and in the process struck up what would become a long relationship with them. Their purpose, they explained, was to get HIV acknowledged by the ACCH as a disease of children, so that parents would have access to more information. They asked how we got there. When we told them that we were just parents who had come on our own, they were impressed. They told us that their group of parents had come on a grant, and Ippy offered to see if we could be reimbursed for our expenses. We thanked her but said that it wasn't necessary. Just in finding out about NIH, we had gotten more than our money's worth.

Ippy told us about an informal meeting of parents of children who had AIDS that they were hosting that evening and invited us to join.

Diana and I couldn't believe what a difference a few hours could make. Just that morning we had been questioning what we were doing there. Now we had hope. After dinner, we met in a large room where about fifty people sat on chairs arranged in a circle. It was both a sad and a welcome sight. For the first time I really felt that I wasn't alone in this. At the same time, though, you couldn't miss the expressions of apprehension and exhaustion. Not sure what to expect, Diana and I took seats next to each other somewhere in the middle.

Ippy introduced herself and gave a brief explanation of what the ACCH was and what it was trying to accomplish. "Now, let's start by going around the room. Each of you stand up and tell us your name and a little bit about why you are here."

The first woman to stand and speak was Louise Ray. She told us that her three sons—Ricky, Robert, and Randy, all hemophiliacs—were infected with HIV through tainted Factor VIII, the blood product that provided the clotting factors hemophiliacs are genetically unable to produce naturally. Her family, which included her husband, Cliff, and a younger daughter, now lived in Sarasota, Florida, and she described how once her boys were diagnosed in 1986, she and her husband did what they considered the responsible, fair thing: They informed the school district in their small rural Florida town. Rather than help her sons, the school district barred the three boys from school, and in 1987, shortly after a court granted them the right to return to school, arsonists burned their home to the ground. Ricky Ray and Ryan White were probably the two most famous children with AIDS at that time. Both they and their families had courageously come forward and spoken out.

As Louise spoke, I sat there amazed. Of course, I had read in the paper about her family's plight, and I'd felt shocked and sympathetic, as any decent person would. But that reaction, as real as it felt, was once removed. I didn't know Louise Ray or her family. To see her actually standing before us, telling her story and opening her heart, made me realize many things. My first thought, one that did not strike me when I heard her story on the news, was, *I'm in the same predicament she's in. That could be me.*

The woman sitting next to Louise rose and told of her little girl, who had contracted HIV through a transfusion during heart surgery. Her daughter could not attend school, and the woman's own family had stopped coming to their home to visit. She described the isolation they now lived with.

A third woman, of West Indian origin, described moving to Florida with her husband, who was, unknown to her, an IV drug user. After he died, she was tested and learned that both she and her baby were infected. Because her family believed that the virus was the result of a hex, everyone she knew refused to associate with her. She had no family or friends, and the only people she could turn to were those with ACCH. One after another, people stood and recounted the discrimination, the isolation, the pain, and even the hatred they were enduring.

I couldn't help but wonder if back in Las Vegas we were all living in some magic bubble that was about to burst. Except for our little run-in with the nursery school, we had received a lot of support from our friends and family. Even the people at my job were generous, never complaining about the extra time I took off, sometimes on a moment's notice. Still, I could not listen to these people and deny their reality. Was this what was in store for us? I was moved by their tears but more struck by the look of absolute bewilderment on their faces, as if HIV and AIDS had crashed them onto a planet light-years removed from everything they knew.

Halfway around the circle, a young, petite white woman with longish hair stood and introduced herself as Elizabeth Glaser. She didn't mention that her husband was Paul Glaser, star of the hit television series *Starsky and Hutch,* and I wasn't a *People* magazine reader then, so I didn't make the connection. She told us how she had received several blood transfusions following the birth of their first child, Ariel. Not only had she herself contracted the virus, but she had passed it on to Ariel through breast-feeding and then on to Ariel's younger brother, Jake. Although Ariel had received intravenous AZT through Dr. Pizzo's program in the last few months of her life and experienced a dramatic improvement, she had died about a year before, in August 1988, a week after her seventh birthday. Now, Elizabeth told us, she was fighting to save Jake. Although she had yet to announce her role in the founding of the Pediatric AIDS Foundation, she and two other women, Susan DeLaurentis and Susie Zeegan, had been working quietly behind the scenes since mid-1988, lobbying politicians and others in positions of influence to do something about pediatric AIDS.

Now, she told us, she was ready to go public. She explained to us that no one outside a close circle of family and friends knew that she, Ariel, and Jake were infected. Although they and everyone around them had gone to great lengths to protect their privacy, the *National Enquirer* was threatening to reveal the real cause of Ariel's death. What I liked about Elizabeth was that she was angry and ready to do something about this terrible injustice. She told us briefly of some of the dirty tactics the tabloid had used to get information on her family, really low stuff such as reporters posing as friends, neighbors, or professional associates to trick those close to them into talking. Elizabeth, however, was one step ahead of them. A press agent working with her family had established enough of a rapport with someone at the *Enquirer* to discover when it planned to publish its revelations about Ariel's death. In the meantime, the Glasers had contacted the *Los Angeles Times* and offered to tell their story. Shortly after the conference, a week before the *Enquirer* planned to break the story, it was scooped by the *L.A. Times* in a story that brought the research-and-treatment crisis in pediatric AIDS to national attention.

I had such admiration for Elizabeth because she was taking back some of the control over her family's life that AIDS had stripped away. Or, I should say, that some people's unenlightened reactions had stripped away. She wasn't running, and she wasn't hiding, although she did tell us that fear of how people would respond to her family forced them to keep their secret as long as they did.

After a couple more people spoke, it was my turn. By then I was emotionally overwhelmed. Though I had begun being more active and assertive in how I dealt with Hydeia's disease, I wasn't totally past the tears quite yet. I wasn't depressed and crying all the time like I had been at the beginning, but I was still vulnerable and raw. Just hearing any one of these people speak would reduce anyone to tears; witnessing over a dozen had me very near my breaking point. Despite the gift of hope and promise I'd received that day, no one could tell me that Hydeia was not going to die.

"Hello, my name is Pat Broadbent. I'm from Las Vegas, Nevada, and I'm here because a year and a half ago my adoptive daughter Hydeia was diagnosed with AIDS. It came to light when her mother gave birth to another child who was HIV-positive more than three years later, and we were advised to have Hydeia tested. Now she is five and she has full-blown AIDS. I came here because there is nothing they can do for her in Las Vegas except treat the illnesses. When I found out about this conference, I felt that maybe I could get more help for her."

I know that I probably said a lot more, but it's hard to remember because about halfway through I was choking back tears and I couldn't breathe through my nose. There was so much emotion in that room, you could almost touch the sadness. When I sat down, it was as if a dam burst. I was crying; my head was pounding; I was a basket case. Diana gently patted my leg, then it was her turn. I've always called her Miss Professional, because she can keep her cool. She explained that she was an educator who had been moved to adopt Hydeia's half brother or brother Mikey because one of the teachers in her school had AIDS. When she heard on the news about Mikey being born HIV-positive without a home to go to, she could not bear the thought of a baby suffering the ostracization her friend had experienced. She called the hospital, then contacted the welfare agency and offered to take him. Unlike me, Diana had some idea of what she was in for. She talked a little bit about how we met, and how Hydeia and Mikey played together, then she sat down.

I was amazed. There was not a tear in her eye. Me? I was still crying. When she leaned over to whisper, "Are you okay?" I snapped under my breath, "Shut up and leave me alone. I'll get it together. Eventually."

After everyone had a chance to share, we stayed for a while and talked. Ippy and Josie invited us to the next conference, and so began a long and productive relationship with the ACCH and some wonderful parents that would result in many positive things in the years to come.

I rode that wave of hope from the conference for weeks. I was ecstatic as I told Dr. K. about Dr. Pizzo, NIH, and the pediatric AIDS protocol. To my surprise, though, he seemed less than enthusiastic about the prospect of Hydeia participating in a clinical trial. "Do you really understand what this will mean for Hydeia?"

"Yeah," I answered impatiently. "She'll be able to get some meds that might keep her alive. At the conference they were saying that these drugs they're giving kids now won't even be on the market for at least two years."

"But do you know what they'll be putting her through?"

"Dr. K., Hydeia is dying. She's already been sick, and she's getting sicker."

He promised to put the papers together, but he asked me to give him a chance to get her in better shape first. That sounded reasonable to me, and I left expecting to hear from NIH any day.

A week or two before the conference, Hydeia had started kindergarten in our neighborhood public school. Despite our experience with the nursery school, I chose to inform her new school of her diagnosis. Unlike the nursery school, our local public school could not refuse Hydeia admission. The legal right of children with HIV and AIDS to attend public schools had been upheld in important lawsuits brought by Ryan White, the Ray family, and other HIV-infected students and their families against school districts across the country. The year before, U.S. surgeon general C. Everett Koop had mailed a pamphlet to more than 100 million homes outlining the facts about AIDS. Looking forward to the first day of school, we believed that the battle against ignorance had been won.

Before Hydeia began school, I talked with the principal, who seemed understanding and supportive. Hydeia's kindergarten teacher welcomed her and was very warm and kind. From the start, I gave them both information from the Centers for Disease Control and other reliable, official sources. It was important that they understood that barring kids making blood pies at recess, there was no way that Hydeia could pass on the virus to another child. HIV was not airborne, and the children's chances of being exposed to infectious bodily fluids—such as vomit, urine, stool, or oral or nasal secretions—was next to nil. Even if a teacher or child was exposed, hand washing would provide sufficient protection. To this day, no one has contracted HIV from an infected person in a child-care center or nursery school. As I had done when Hydeia was in nursery school, I reminded the school administrators and teachers how important it was that she not be exposed to infection from other children.

On several occasions I even offered to speak with the other parents, but the principal thought it best to keep the information confidential. Perhaps she was concerned about alarming other parents, but I didn't see it that way. Because we had always dealt with Hydeia having AIDS in a calm, matter-of-fact way, she had no problem sharing her diagnosis with anyone. I expected her to talk about it with her classmates, so the news was bound to get out to the other kids. I thought the principal was naïve to think none of Hydeia's classmates would share this information with their parents. From the beginning, I've always felt that the most important aspect of sharing information about HIV/AIDS is controlling who says what to whom and when. My talking to the parents, I could control. What I didn't want to contend with was parents who got the news from their five-year-old and then panicked before they had the facts. Unfortunately, this decision was not mine.

Hydeia's teacher was kind and supportive, and Hydeia adored her. Little by little, however, it became clear that her teacher was having some problems with Hydeia being there. I started getting calls and requests to meet with the teacher and the principal to discuss how to "handle" Hydeia. Then came meetings with the school nurse. At that time the information on HIV and AIDS was rapidly evolving, and what you read one place might contradict what you read somewhere else. Hydeia's teacher would fixate on these discrepancies. Rather than quell her obsession with how the virus was spread, the information just seemed to feed it. Each new discovery about HIV supported the safety of casual contact. For some reason, though, that message was not getting through to her.

Before long it seemed that every other question began with the words "What if?" As in, What if another student who bites his fingernails or has a hangnail goes to help Hydeia when she's bleeding? The "what if" scenarios became more complicated and far-fetched. Beyond pointing out that such scenarios were extremely unlikely to occur and if they did, I trusted the staff to have the good sense to protect any of the children from exposure to Hydeia's blood, I reminded them of a few other facts. First, for all they knew, Hydeia was not the only child in the school, or even in her class, who was HIV-positive. Second, there were possibly children carrying a hepatitis virus, which is thousands of times more easily transmitted and in some cases lethal. Third, the person most at risk in that classroom was Hydeia herself. Yes, yes, she would answer, as if everything I had been saying the past few months was finally sinking in. But it never did.

One day Hydeia came home from school with a huge bandage covering her upper forearm, her elbow, and part of her upper arm. From the looks of it, you'd think she'd been shot. "What happened to your elbow?" I asked. She told me that she had fallen and scraped it on the playground. Of course, then she did what she had seen all the other kids do: rinse it off in the water fountain. Her teacher must have seen her fall, because as Hydeia walked casually to the fountain, her teacher chased after her screaming, "Stop, Hydeia! Don't put your arm in the fountain!"

"And, Mommy," Hydeia said proudly, "I didn't."

"Okay, good for you," I said, the whole time picturing this teacher hauling butt across the playground in a panic.

Hydeia's teacher phoned me early one evening shortly before Christmas. We were all going to see Keisha perform in her school's Christmas recital and were literally walking out the door when the phone rang. After a few minutes, I knew this conversation wasn't ending anytime soon. I signaled to Loren and the kids to go ahead without me, I would catch up. For the next three hours I listened as Hydeia's teacher explained that she would be happy to teach Hydeia at home. I told her that that was not an option, since there was no medical reason for Hydeia not to be in school. The teacher responded with a series of hypothetical scenarios in which my baby might infect another child. I repeated what I'd already said a hundred times: "If HIV were that easy to catch, my entire family would be infected. We aren't. Doesn't that tell you something?" I asked, exasperated. The more I listened, the more ridiculous she sounded. Finally I said, "If the ceiling falls in, what are you going to tell the parents? You cannot even educate yourself about this. How can you expect to educate anyone else?"

She had no answer to that, but she did say that she worried what would happen to her if another parent found out that her child had been "exposed" to HIV by being in Hydeia's class. After all, she added, her husband was a lawyer and he was concerned that another parent might hold her liable for not informing them about Hydeia. I reminded her, firmly, that in discussing Hydeia with anyone, including her husband, she had breached confidentiality. Ironically, that same confidentiality prevented me from sharing the information with parents from the start, like I'd wanted to. But that was another issue.

Three hours later Loren and the kids came home, and there I was, still in my coat, trying to calm down Hydeia's teacher. I realized that nothing I said would make a difference. Hydeia continued going to school, and whenever she was in the hospital (which was often that year), her teacher would visit her. Though I wasn't happy about the situation, I reminded myself that Hydeia had only half a school year to go and that the teacher had not done anything to really hurt her.

One day Hydeia was standing next to me while I was loading the washer full of whites. I poured in the soap powder, and when I began pouring in the bleach, Hydeia reflexively covered her eyes with both hands.

"What are you doing?" I asked.

"That burns my eyes!"

I was confused. "It's burning your eyes *now?*"

"No, one day, Mommy, I sneezed and boogies went all over the table. And the teacher got a bottle and was spraying all around." Hydeia waved her hand in the air around her face. "Then she sprayed the table and cleaned it up. But the spray burned my eyes, and it smelled just like that." She pointed to the bleach. It took me a second to figure out what had happened. Then I hit the roof.

I called Loren at work and told him that I was going up to the school. "Pat, you act so crazy when get angry," he warned.

"I know, but I think she needs to realize that she's crossed the line." Loren promised to come pick me up, but after an hour passed (maybe he thought I would cool down and let it pass) and he wasn't there, I walked up to the school myself.

I went to the principal and said, "You need to come with me."

"Mrs. Broadbent, what's the matter?"

"I'll let you learn about it the same way I learned about it. Come down to Hydeia's classroom." The principal followed me to the classroom door. I knocked, and her teacher answered. "I understand that Hydeia sneezed and you sprayed her with bleach."

"No, no. What I did was—she sneezed and mucus went everywhere, and I just didn't know what to do. So I had bleach and water here because the pamphlet you gave me said you should clean up things with bleach diluted with water."

"Yes," I said.

"And so, she sneezed, and they were in a little reading group at the reading table, so I sprayed the table, and then I sprayed a little in the air around her."

"It's not airborne," I snapped, stunned. "Why were you spraying the air? If it were airborne, she wouldn't be in school. If I thought other people could get infected that way, I wouldn't let her around anyone."

I was upset, and she was flustered. All she could offer was her usual "I have these other students here. I just feel responsible." When she showed me how she had sprayed the air around Hydeia, I grabbed her finger and held it in my hand. "If you ever spray my baby again, I will take this finger and I will break it. Do you understand me?"

She just looked at me.

"You did more damage spraying Hydeia in the eyes than she could have ever done to anyone just by sneezing." I let go of her finger, then turned to the principal. "Do you have any questions?"

"I'm sorry—" she started, but I was walking away. It was one thing to be ignorant. After you get the information, then you have no excuse for acting ignorant. If you keep acting like this after you know the facts, then you're just stupid.

Hydeia never got bleach sprayed in her face again, but she did come home and casually tell me things suggesting that the problem continued. Once when she accidentally piddled on the floor, the teacher insisted the janitor put on gloves before he mopped it up—despite the fact that urine does not contain the virus, despite the fact that he was using a mop and wouldn't be touching it anyway. Fortunately for Hydeia, she was too young to understand the fear and the ignorance behind this behavior. She loved her teacher so much, and I never said anything to make her feel otherwise. However, when she asked me to cut a rose from one of my rosebushes to take to school, I did so gritting my teeth. Oddly enough, it never occurred to me to ask for a different teacher or take Hydeia out of school. One teacher or another— I didn't expect it to make much difference. Going to school and having friends were normal parts of life I wanted Hydeia to experience for as long as she could.

Still, it bothered me that a child—or anyone—faced with a terminal disease had to put up with the neurotic fears of people who could not accept the facts. True, there was always misinformation floating out there, and the media often sensationalized anything about HIV and AIDS. However, while the experts did not know everything, by 1989 they did know about all there was to know about how HIV was transmitted. On top of the truly serious things we had to deal with, it made me furious to be wasting time and energy answering questions that everybody should have known the answer to. What made it even more frightening was that Hydeia was not just some child her teacher had read about. She knew her, and she knew me. I had held her hand and walked her through everything she needed to know to protect herself and her students from the risk that did not exist. Clearly, whatever education people were receiving was not enough. Much more needed to be done.

Several months had passed since the pediatric AIDS conference, and we were no closer to getting to NIH. In January, when Diana went to NIH with Mikey, she asked around and discovered that Hydeia's paperwork had not arrived in Bethesda. When she told me, I felt betrayed. Hydeia had gotten sick again, and Dr. K. seemed reluctant to send the paperwork while she was sick. That didn't make any sense to me. Each illness was, to me, a reason to push the process of getting her to NIH, not a reason not to. The next time Dr. K. tried to explain this to me, I said, "Listen. You have been taking care of Hydeia for two and a half years. It's not your fault that no one knows what they're doing with these kids. But at least if I get her up to NIH, she'll be cared for by the people who know the most. She will get AZT, and they have a new protocol for CD4 and one for ddI that she might qualify for. I want her to get the drugs. I don't think she'll be here much longer if I don't take her."

By then Tiffany had become extremely ill. We tried to help her grandmother get her up to NIH, too, but it was too late. Of the three remaining children in Las Vegas, Hydeia was the oldest, and I could not help wondering if she would be next. She spent most of January and February in the hospital, with one wave of infection after another pounding her little body. How much longer could she hold out?

It was around this time that the first child with AIDS that I knew or knew of passed away. Tiffany was one of the first five children diagnosed in Las Vegas, and the second to die. Looking back, I don't think I gave the decision to attend Tiffany's funeral a lot of thought. Being a parent of a child with AIDS thrusts you into a community of other parents, grandparents, and caregivers who were living the same nightmare. We did try to support one another, sometimes I guess to make up for all the other people who turned their backs. At the time, I suppose I saw attending a child's funeral as a gesture of support. As I sat at the back of the funeral home and looked at Tiffany's frail body in the coffin, it was almost like I was hallucinating. Suddenly the little white blond girl turned into a little black girl—Hydeia. I held on as long as I could before excusing myself and leaving. I vowed never to attend another funeral or memorial service again. Though I know the presence of friends can lend support to families in a time of need, for me it felt like a rehearsal for the one funeral I knew I would not avoid.

I could feel time running out like sand through my fingers. My sole focus became getting my baby to NIH. There was no question but that Dr. K. cared for Hydeia and wanted to protect her. Like most people then, he probably believed that she was going to die eventually anyway. Why put her through the frequent flights to Bethesda? The tests and procedures? The potentially serious side effects of these new, toxic medications?

"You know, Pat," he said once, "she'll be like a guinea pig."

"You know what, Dr. K.? She *is* a guinea pig, no matter where she goes, because no one knows what they're doing and we're always trying this and trying that. At least if she goes to NIH, she'll be a guinea pig who is getting state-of-the-art care and a chance. Now, I want her papers sent up to NIH, and I want it done right now."

Dr. K. promised to cooperate. Walking away, I tried to see his side. I tried to imagine how I might feel if the treatments I was praying would save her life actually made things worse for her. My mind always stopped with the question, Worse than what? The death that grew more certain with every setback? Nothing could be worse than that.

Finally, in February 1990, we got the call from NIH: Hydeia could come. Cindy got her call at the same time, so we booked our flights together. Cindy and I both felt anxious and excited. I remember looking out the plane window as we landed. If there was any hope in the world, it was right here.

THREE

*I*t's funny to think back on how unforgettable that first trip to NIH was. Little did I know that for the next twelve years, catching a flight between Las Vegas and Washington, D.C., would become as routine as driving to work. The six-hour trip (complete with stopovers) would get us into Washington very late. By the time we'd get our luggage, it would be close to midnight, and by the time we'd take a cab to our hotel in Bethesda, closer to 1 A.M. In addition to carrying Hydeia, who sometimes didn't have the stamina to walk, I had the luggage, her nebulizer for the LIP, the solutions for the nebulizer, and her stroller-style wheelchair. Between the travel and the three-hour time difference, we would have appreciated a couple of hours' extra sleep, but we had to be up at seven in the morning. We would bundle the kids into a cab for the ride to NIH, feed (or try to feed) them in the hospital cafeteria, and have them ready for the first tests and appointments at nine. Looking back now, I wonder how I did it. Then, of course, that thought never crossed my mind.

The National Institutes of Health is located on a large, beautifully landscaped campus outside Bethesda. Since that first morn-

MY POEM

Family and friends are important, especially when you have a deadly disease. I am going to tell you about my life. I have AIDS and I am very important to my mommy and daddy and all the rest of the people that know that I have AIDS. Some kids don't understand that if they play with me they cannot get AIDS. Some kids even know more than their parents. When I have a new friend and she or he finds out I have AIDS and they do not know a lot about it, I will help them understand. My life is fun because I have a big sister who understands a lot. It is also fun because I have friends who will play with me a lot. I like to educate people. I have two very special friends. One helps me a lot when I need her. That is Lori. And the other one acts like a kid even though she is grown. But I do like that in people. That is Trish. But my very very special friend is my mom. She helps me when I need her, and I help her when she needs me. Even though I might die before her, I will never stop loving her and she will never stop loving me. Educating people helps me make a lot of friends. This poem is not like others because the others that I have written help educate people. This one tells you how I feel. Thank you for listening. The end.

Hydeia
Age eight

ing in March 1990, our world has revolved around the thirteenth floor, east, of the Clinical Center. It is here that all of the routine tests and procedures are done. When Hydeia's condition has required hospitalization, we have been in the western wing of the thirteenth floor. (It's a good thing I'm not superstitious.) You would never imagine calling a hospital a second home, but that is exactly what NIH became for us. NIH is not only the place where Hydeia's life would be saved—more than once—but also a community of dedicated, caring doctors, nurses, and staff. It was also where Hydeia and I both made friends we will treasure for a lifetime.

When you see a place the size of NIH and think about allowing your child to take part in a clinical study, you naturally wonder if she will be treated as a case number and not a child. By the time Cindy and I arrived in Bethesda, we had heard Diana raving about her and Mikey's experience there. Still, you never know. Many things about NIH impressed me, but none more than its commitment to the needs of the entire family. Our first day there, we met our social worker, Lori Wiener. Warm, caring, and easy to talk to, Lori impressed me as the type of person who would go that extra mile for you. In all the years I've known her, she has never failed to live up to that first impression. Lori is still our social worker at NIH, and I consider her a friend. Her concern for the entire family and the problems we have faced beyond the NIH campus has often made me reflect on my time as a social worker and hope that my clients felt the same care and nonjudgmental support I have always felt with Lori. As the first human face we encountered at NIH, Lori welcomed Cindy, Hydeia, Tyler, and me downstairs, helped us sign in, and then brought us upstairs, where we met with doctors.

One doctor described the types of studies they were doing and what it meant to be "on protocol." The purpose of the protocols and the extensive testing our kids would undergo was twofold. First, obviously, to give our children the advantage of the newest information and treatment. Second, the doctors at NIH literally were writing the book on how to treat children with HIV and AIDS. At that time, if a child showed up with a life-threatening case of PCP or one of the many more "exotic" opportunistic infections, the average doctor was pretty much on her own. There was no database or textbook to which a doctor could turn to determine, for example, the correct dosage of medications that for the most part had never been tested or approved for use in children.

Few doctors were in a position to see a number of these children, and much of the research and information that existed pertained to adults with HIV/AIDS and simply did not apply to children. Medically speaking, children are not simply small adults. Their developing bodies and minds are different in countless ways, and because they are still growing, they are vulnerable to adverse reactions to medication and treatment. Take, for example, the logical assumption that children always require less of a given medication to achieve the same effect. The surprising truth is that because children's bodies metabolize, or use and break down, medications at different rates, they may really require more, or a different schedule.

HIV and AIDS do not always behave the same way in children and adults. Being born with HIV or being infected as a child creates problems for children that those who contract the virus as adults do not encounter: stunted physical growth and developmental delays, as well as beginning life with an already compromised immune system. For example, children rarely develop Kaposi's sarcoma, an opportunistic skin cancer that is one of the major early signs of AIDS in adult males. (In fact, early in the epidemic, some medical experts and policy makers took the absence of Kaposi's in children as proof that their bizarre immune deficiencies were not caused by the same agent that caused AIDS.) Children differ from adults in other ways, too. For example, when the virus crosses into the brain, it causes dementia and neuropathy (changes and disturbances in brain and nerve function). In adults, this is usually irreversible, even with AZT. However, among the surprise results of early pediatric trials was that AZT could reverse symptoms of neuropathy. Dr. Pizzo's group discovered that for some children, AZT in pill form was not absorbed sufficiently, whereas receiving the drug intravenously could produce significant improvements.

Finally, in those days the treatment of these children was complicated by the fact that the vast majority had additional serious health issues. The hemophiliacs who contracted the virus through Factor VIII already had one life-threatening disease. Children like Hydeia, who contracted the virus before or at birth, may also have been exposed to nicotine, alcohol, and illicit drugs in the womb—any of which can cause other problems with physical health and mental development. Many of these babies also suffered from a lack of prenatal care, inadequate prenatal nutrition, and little or no medical care after birth.

We also learned the practical aspects of our participation in the protocol. First, the cost of Hydeia's care—including meds, treatment, tests, and hospitalization—was covered by NIH. Because the pharmaceutical company that creates a drug must submit it to clinical trials before it can be approved by the Food and Drug Administration and sold in the United States, the company may underwrite study participants' miscellaneous expenses. After the first trip, a pharmaceutical company would cover the costs of our air travel, while NIH gave us a per diem allowance for hotel and meal costs. (Our private insurance and Medicaid covered Hydeia's medical expenses in Las Vegas.) If we required anything that local doctors or medical facilities could not provide, NIH would help. When the Las Vegas home health team that mixed one of Hydeia's medications lacked a necessary piece of equipment, NIH shipped it right out.

Second, we had to agree that we would follow the rules and restrictions of the protocol faithfully, because to do otherwise would taint or invalidate the data. We were charged with keeping meticulous records on all aspects of our kids' health: the schedule and dosage of medications, any side effects, fevers, other symptoms we noticed, and so on. In the event that a child suddenly fell ill at home and was treated or hospitalized there, NIH had to be kept abreast of what was happening. It was important to the study that our children's health care team at home be willing to run tests, do procedures, and collect information that, while not medically necessary, NIH might request. We were told that in case of a medical crisis, if at all possible, the child should be brought to NIH.

Third, we had to follow the schedule for visits to the tee, understanding that NIH could make no promises about how long each visit might be and what it might entail. For instance, during the first three months after our first visit, we flew to NIH every week. Over time, the schedule would change to every other week for the next twelve weeks, then every three weeks. For the past six years or so, we have gone once every twelve weeks. Of course, that was the best-case-scenario schedule. If Hydeia's NIH doctors were satisfied with how she looked and the test results, she would be cleared to go home. However, if there was ever the slightest indication that something was not right, we had to stay. That might mean an extra day or an extra month. Or two. The way the protocol worked, if you were scheduled to be at NIH every other Wednesday and one visit lasted ten days, you were still due back the following Wednesday. I can count on one hand the number of "routine" visits we had those first several years. Our first visit—which should have been two weeks long—ran closer to four.

While any parent would do anything to save her child, I didn't have to spend too much time at NIH to see that you needed more than love and hope to stick with the protocol. You needed an understanding spouse capable of running a household. You needed children who could manage without Mom around for days or weeks at a time without falling apart. You needed devoted, selfless family, friends, and neighbors willing to pitch in on a moment's notice to do anything and everything from feed and walk your dog to take in your sick child's sibling (or siblings) for a few days if your spouse had to rush to NIH in a crisis. You needed either the financial security for one of you to stop working or an understanding employer who would tolerate the unexpected absences, latenesses, and interruptions. I was fortunate to have been working for Lettica, a printing company, then. To say that there was nothing my boss and coworkers would not do to accommodate my family doesn't begin to tell the story. When I did finally quit, later in 1991, my employer offered to continue my health insurance coverage long beyond the period required by law.

Finally, I agreed that if my child died, whether at NIH or anyplace else, her body would be autopsied at NIH, with the program covering all expenses. While as a parent you couldn't help but view NIH as a place of potential miracles, you also had to be realistic. Saving our children's lives and the lives of others was its mission. However, to fulfill that mission, the doctors and researchers needed information to understand exactly what was going on inside each child. I soon learned how quickly this disease could spin around on you and how easily a child could go down. Though the cause of AIDS was established, how it worked remained an endlessly shifting kaleidoscope of mysteries.

In the event of her death, in exchange for granting NIH its last chance to study my baby, she would be sent home "burial-ready," a term that is as jarring to write today as it was to hear then. No matter how much I believed that I had accepted the possibility that Hydeia might die, the image of her coming home in a coffin in the cargo underbelly of a jet struck me with the force of lightning. I vowed then that I would do everything in my power to see to it that Hydeia always came home, as I like to say, riding in the top of the plane, beside me.

By that point, NIH had reviewed Hydeia's medical records

and assured me that she probably qualified for the study. Over the next few days Hydeia had every possible test you can imagine. In addition to the routine blood and urine tests, she underwent an EKG, CAT scan, spinal tap, echocardiogram, MRI, chest X ray, and other diagnostic tests, including a pulmonary-function test for which we had to make the short trip to Children's Hospital in Washington. At that time, Hydeia was still sucking on a pacifier. Granted, she was a little bit old for it, but weaning her from the comfort it provided wasn't even on my list of priorities. When a nurse insisted that it be removed before an MRI, I refused and asked why.

"Well, it will compromise the image," she replied.

"You mean to tell me a doctor who's an expert at reading an MRI won't be able to tell by the shape that this is a pacifier in her mouth?"

The nurse said nothing, and Hydeia kept her pacifier. It reminded me that the lessons I'd learned back in Las Vegas about staying on top of everything still applied.

With a T-cell count below 150 and a history of opportunistic infections, Hydeia qualified for a study Dr. Pizzo was conducting on recombinant CD4. Occurring naturally in the body, CD4 cells are a critical component of the immune system that HIV can decimate. Hydeia would be given a new, manmade substance resulting from genetically combining a portion of CD4 with a portion of a human antibody molecule. Early laboratory studies had suggested that recombinant CD4 could prevent the virus from infecting healthy cells by "trapping" it. No one was certain if recombinant CD4 would act the same way in a human body. This was a phase I study, which meant that its goal was to establish safety and dose ranges. Hydeia would be one of twenty-six children receiving a continuous infusion of CD4 (as opposed to periodic infusions or injections). The idea was to try CD4 alone first, then in a month or so add ddI, the antiviral drug related to AZT.

It sounded promising, but even without knowing if the CD4 worked, I had great confidence in the care she would receive. Dr. Pizzo and his staff worked as a team, and everyone always knew what was going on with each child. This was a welcome change from the situation we—and most other families—faced in their community hospitals, where your child's care was a patchwork of different doctors, specialties, and philosophies. When Hydeia was hospitalized for her sinus infection or a bout of PCP, we would have Dr. K. as well as numerous other specialists all approaching the current crisis like the proverbial blind men and the elephant. With the exception of Dr. K., none of them had the background or experience to see the big picture. The lack of coordination made for a frustrating, anxiety-provoking, not to mention potentially dangerous, situation.

What I loved about the NIH staff was that everyone who dealt with Hydeia had the same information. Decisions were group decisions that took into account the many facets of this complex disease. Clearly, Dr. Pizzo set the tone. I swear, he must have memorized the results of every test these kids had. The other thing about Dr. Pizzo that I will never forget was his accessibility and warmth. He was always approachable. If you had a question, a concern, a complaint, or a comment, he listened.

For Hydeia to start on the CD4 protocol, it was necessary that she have a Hickman catheter surgically implanted into a large vein in her chest. Dr. K. had been trying to persuade me to get Hydeia a Hickman for some time. I knew that it would save her not only the discomfort of repeated needle sticks for administering medication and taking blood but damage to the veins themselves. (Veins subjected to repeated injections can harden, shrink, or collapse, making them difficult or impossible to access for future use.) Using a central venous catheter like the Hickman offered many advantages. Because it was "attached" to a larger vein in the neck or, in Hydeia's case, the chest, larger quantities of fluids and medication could be administered instantly in case of an emergency. In addition, the larger veins were not as sensitive as the smaller arm and leg veins to irritation from medication or from intravenous feeding. Since Hydeia's nutritional status remained an ongoing concern, there was a real possibility that she might require intravenous feeding in the near future. While intellectually I understood Dr. K.'s reasoning and hated to see Hydeia suffer, I hadn't been able to do it. To me, the Hickman symbolized the severity of her illness, one of the last "stops" en route to the end. Kids who had central venous catheters were the ones closest to death, and it was difficult for me to see Hydeia that way.

Prior to getting the Hickman, Hydeia had had a port, which is another kind of central venous line, but with an access area that is right under the skin and nearly invisible. The problem with the port was that it was so uncomfortable for Hydeia whenever someone tried to access it. She told me she would rather get stuck in the arm fifty times, and how she would scream and carry on. Even when we talked her through it, it would take a couple of adults to hold her down. She couldn't stand it, and to be honest, I didn't have the stomach for it either.

When it was time to have the catheter implanted, I briefly explained to Hydeia what the doctors were going to do. As always, her main question was, "Will I be asleep?" I assured her that she would be, and she was fine. When it came to Hydeia's condition and what was happening medically, I tried to be open without overwhelming her with unnecessary information. I called this my "need to know" policy. My first, natural inclination was always to try to emotionally "defuse" these situations for Hydeia by being as calm and as matter-of-fact about them as I could. Children are masters at cracking the code of how we act, regardless of what we say. I knew that saying to Hydeia "Everything's going to be okay" while I choked back tears wasn't going to cut it. Regardless of how I felt, I never let Hydeia know it. Not only did I believe it's the parent's responsibility to set the tone for a child, I'd been around enough parents whose children had HIV/AIDS to see how much more the children suffered—emotionally and physically—when Mom or Dad failed to keep it together.

The first time I saw Hydeia with the Hickman in place, it looked so foreign and intimidating. Protruding from a hole in the upper right side of her tiny chest were a few inches of flexible tubing with a plastic cap, or lumen. That is where you would insert a syringe for a regular injection or attach more tubing for a more permanent connection for continuous infusion. Despite the clear advantages of the Hickman, it demanded scrupulous sterile procedure and entailed some potential risks as well. The most serious, of course, was infection, because an infection that entered through the Hickman went straight to the blood and could be fatal. Anytime a new infusion or injection was introduced, there was a risk that air entering the line could cause a fatal embolism. Blood clots could also form on the body side of the port. To prevent that, you had to learn to flush the line with heparin, an anticlotting medicine, to dissolve any clots before they either blocked the vein or broke off and traveled to the heart, lungs, or brain, where they could be fatal.

Having a child on protocol meant getting a crash course in what I'd call hard-core nursing. After all, outside the walls of NIH, we would be mixing the meds, managing and programming the computerized pump that delivered them through the catheter, attaching the pump to the Hickman, flushing the line, keeping the port area sterile, and learning to instantly recognize and manage problems. Intellectually, I understood all this when I consented to have the Hickman implanted, but it wasn't until a nurse was teaching Cindy and me how to actually do all this that the awesome responsibility crashed down. If I screwed up one step, let my guard down for a millisecond, Hydeia could become critically ill, even die. The people at NIH made it clear that no child on protocol could leave until they were satisfied that the parent had mastered these procedures. I remember looking at the pump and saying to one nurse, "Do you realize that I don't even know how to program my VCR?" By the time I left NIH, however, I felt I could probably program the entire ballistic-missile system.

The procedure, which had to be followed precisely every time, took about forty-five minutes a day after I'd mastered it. In the beginning it took a lot longer. Once you started it, you couldn't stop until it was complete, so you had to line up all of your supplies—wastebasket, alcohol, sterile gauze pads, povidone iodine (PVP) swabsticks, hydrogen peroxide, sterile Q-tips, and PVP swabs. That was just to do a routine dressing change. To inject the heparin, you needed to line up your syringes, sterile gauze pads, new cap, and alcohol swabs. Each step of each procedure became like a ritual. You scrubbed the site with PVP for exactly three minutes in a circular motion, moving from the center gradually outward in increasingly larger circles, then wiped it up with gauze soaked in hydrogen peroxide, then dried it with more sterile gauze, then wiped the catheter from bottom to top with a PVP swab. And this was just one step of dozens. Everything had to be perfectly sterile. If you rubbed your nose at any point or touched anything that was not sterile, you had to start again. Even the vial the heparin came in had to be cleaned with alcohol before you filled the syringe. There was no rushing, no cutting corners.

Then there was the pump that supplied the recombinant CD4 and ddI, which had to be set to deliver exactly the right amount of medicine over a period. I have pictures of me sitting on the bed in the hospital with the pump in my hand, trying to coax the darned thing into starting. For some reason, Cindy thought this was funny enough to warrant a picture. As I learned early on, if you didn't learn to laugh at something about your time at what I'd begun to call "the finishing school of pediatric AIDS," you would go mad. My sister Joyce sewed a bunch of different backpacks and we bought little purses that Hydeia carried the pump in wherever she went, including to sleep. It never came off. Over time, Loren and the older kids learned how to program the pump and what to do if it started beeping or acting crazy (we always had spares available). Eventually Hydeia could even administer her own injections and draw her own blood through the Hickman.

I know some parents found such intensive participation in their child's care empowering, but I never did. The way I saw it, I had no choice. This disease was spinning all of our lives out of control. I was determined to grab all the control I could, however I could. Sure, we could have had a crew of nurses in and out the door several times a day, but that was impractical. You couldn't have a child on a twenty-four-hour system and depend on other people to come running every time the pump beeped or the site around the line looked inflamed. Like so much about living with AIDS, like so much about being a parent, you just did it. We did have a wonderful nurse named Harlene Farrell, who worked and traveled with us for several years.

After three and a half weeks at NIH, Hydeia was cleared to go home. On every trip we had to carry home the meds, equipment, and other supplies, including the sterile distilled water used to dilute some of the meds before they were infused. I remember struggling through the airport and onto the plane weighted down with luggage, shopping bags full of medical stuff, and Hydeia. The first few times, it was an adventure. Within a few months, every pilot, flight attendant, and ticket officer on either end of the trip knew Hydeia and me by name. Before too long, the flight attendants were letting Hydeia stand in the aisle and give the preflight safety demonstration, which she knew by heart.

Back home, we quickly fell into the new routines of caring for Hydeia, traveling back and forth from NIH, and getting Hydeia's doctors, mainly Dr. K., into working with NIH, too. I started keeping a notebook that I stored in the dining room buffet, along with all of the medical supplies. In it I wrote down all kinds of information about the meds she was taking, the dosages, problems or changes, her temperature, and so on.

Obviously, it was great to be back home with Loren and Keisha. We had missed them so much, and it was such a comfort knowing Loren took such great care of Keisha, who was about eight then. Regardless of how Loren and I tried to split our attention between the two girls evenly, there was no doubt that Hydeia often got the lion's share. Keisha loved Hydeia and was so protective of her. She understood what AIDS was and what it meant. Although our family philosophy was that if someone had a problem with AIDS, that was their problem, not ours, we were honest with Keisha when we talked to her about telling her friends. Some of them might not like it, or their parents might not let them come over to play at our house. Of course, we hoped that wouldn't happen, but she had to be prepared if it did. Keisha decided to tell her friends about it anyway, because she also wanted to make people understand. Kendall, Pepe, and Kimmie were always ready to help at home, or to travel with us, when needed.

The bond Diana, Cindy, and I shared grew even stronger, as we sometimes traveled together to or from NIH, shared hotel rooms and endless hours. During this time we began working on our dream—a day-care center and school for children with HIV/AIDS and their siblings. The seeds were first sown when Diana heard about Michael that New Year's Day in 1987, when all he was to any of us was a baby on the news who had no home. My own experience with Hydeia's nursery school convinced me that something needed to be done. Having found our ways to NIH, the three of us knew all too well that when it came to kids with AIDS, if you wanted anything done for your child, you had to be prepared to do it yourself. We agreed on a name for our dream: Reach Out, an acronym for Relieving Every AIDS Child's Hurt is Our Ultimate Task.

We began by doing public speaking in and around Las Vegas, trying to pique some interest and support in creating the center and also to raise awareness about AIDS. By then we were veterans of numerous ACCH conferences and experienced in leading support groups and helping other parents. In our presentations, the three of us would each tell our stories, but I guess we didn't come across as emotionally as people expected because we didn't get too much of a response. With a few exceptions, neither we three nor our kids had been discriminated against, ostracized, or as badly treated as Ryan White, the Ray family, or some others. We were three women determined to be in control, and by then I guess you could say that our pity party was over. Sure, we each had moments, and we often turned to one another for a shoulder to cry on. However, to the outside world, we probably came across a bit too businesslike, so we shifted our focus and started speaking to people on a more personal level. The numbers of children infected with HIV were rising, and these were only the ones who had been diagnosed. It was like the tip of an iceberg, we warned audiences. Then we asked them to think about how they would feel if it was their child being discriminated against or ostracized because they had a fatal disease. We asked them to imagine knowing that their child could die at any time and then having to fight for even the most basic help and understanding. This struck the right chord, and people responded. We began collecting funds, as well as promises of assistance with everything from helping to find a location to providing supplies.

Though the primary focus of my energies during these years would be Hydeia, I also saw AIDS in a wider context than just what it was doing to my baby and to our family. Sitting in that circle with those other families at that first conference, I saw firsthand the toll public fear and ignorance were taking. But that was only a couple of hours. Up at NIH, I met and got to know many other parents, mostly mothers, who were coping with their child's AIDS without the support Diana, Cindy, and I had.

Because I was a trained social worker and had dealt with people in crisis, I couldn't help but "study" what I saw and try to learn from it. Coping with HIV/AIDS is devastating for any family, and some parents were better than others at protecting their children from seeing the collateral damage—the lost jobs, the financial difficulties, the crumbling marriages, and so on.

The experience of battling HIV/AIDS too often involved social isolation, for both the kids and the parents or other caregivers. It also meant that lots of these kids spent more time around adults than around kids their own age, so some of them grew up fast. Hydeia was definitely such a child. Though she had always had solid self-esteem and an independent streak, living with HIV/AIDS exposed her to so many adults that she seemed years older than she was, even though her small size made her appear years younger. In some ways, kids like Hydeia were a lot quicker to pick up on how we parents really felt and what we really meant. In terms of the resources and support we had, we were certainly luckier than many families I would meet. But that didn't mean that this HIV/AIDS stuff wasn't making all of our lives hell at times. More than once, just hours before our plane was to leave for Vegas, we got the news that Hydeia needed to stay. Though later, alone in my room, I might cry or curse in frustration, Hydeia never saw that. The last thing she and the other kids at NIH needed was to feel that their parents' or their families' problems were their fault.

Yet, sadly, I saw parents who just could not maintain that boundary. At their child's bedside, a father might worriedly wonder aloud if he'd be fired for taking another day off, or a mother might complain about having to stay longer. There were others—not many, though—who complained about the rigors and inconvenience of keeping to the protocol. Even among those who had no problems with the program, there were kids whose own families did not even know they had the virus. One mother I know had her whole family convinced that her child had leukemia. These kids were forced to take their meds in a closet or the laundry room, where no one—not even other family members—would see them. Some parents would take the AIDS drugs out of their original prescription bottles and put them in other bottles, so no one would know what the child was taking. I remember hearing one boy speak at a conference about knowing that he had AIDS and yet having to listen to family members and friends speak with fear and hatred of people with AIDS.

Unfortunately, kids like these got the message that they and their disease were a burden, a problem, a pain, an embarrassment, a shame. When parents would tell me something like this, I'd want to shake them and scream, "Is this how you want your child to spend what could be the last days of his life?" But I never did. The forces some of these parents confronted back in their hometowns, sometimes even within the walls of their own homes, I wouldn't presume to understand. However, it seemed to me that rather than stand up to the ignorance, too many were going along with it, although they knew it was wrong. In my opinion, they were putting their fear of other people's stupidity before their child's right to live whatever life she had free of shame and fear, free of knowing that others believed she was to blame for her disease or that there was something "dirty" about having it. Some parents would acknowledge that this was probably the wrong thing to do, and they resented having to do it. Of course, I wasn't naïve. I knew how people could be, but to me that seemed to give them even less of a right to dictate the terms of my child's life. When people went along with something they knew to be wrong, I called it "cosigning the bullshit." Loren and I taught our kids that this was something we just did not do, for anyone. I vowed never to let that happen when it came to Hydeia.

Another reason it was so important to us that Hydeia learn to accept her AIDS without shame or self-pity had to do with color. In a strange way, when it came to dealing with all this, I found being black gave me a different perspective. As far as being discriminated against and judged unfairly went, I, like most black Americans, had had more than enough experience. I remember sitting up at NIH talking to a white mother about how badly people were treating her family because of the AIDS. White, well-off, and professional, this woman had grown up in a privileged world where she was treated with courtesy and respect. When her child was diagnosed with AIDS, that all changed. Suddenly people she knew and people she didn't were asking questions, making assumptions, and judging her and her family. "Can you imagine?" she would ask, recounting the latest injustice. I sat listening, all the while thinking, *Yes, I can.*

As a mother whom Hydeia recently described to a journalist as someone who "wore Afros in the sixties and burned her bra," I knew my daughter came into this world with two strikes against her. There was no way anyone was ever going to make her doubt her self-worth just because she had this disease. Around our house, we talked about there being two kinds of people in the world: those who were ignorant and those who were stupid. Ignorant people didn't know any better, we told Hydeia, but if you explained things like AIDS to them, they might decide to learn. On the other hand, some people were stupid. They were the ignorant people who continued acting stupid even after they knew the truth. "And we don't want to be around people like that, do we?" I'd ask, and she'd shake her little head.

Before she was six, Hydeia knew the difference between ignorance and stupidity, and she had no problem pointing it out. Years later, when Hydeia began speaking publicly, there were some who wondered if somebody else was putting words in her mouth. Believe me, Hydeia's got plenty of her own words and ideas; she doesn't need anyone else's. She had many friends at NIH whose parents made them keep secrets, whose parents taught them to feel afraid and unworthy. Early on, when Hydeia was asked why she spoke out, she would reply, "Because I want kids to be able to say, 'I have AIDS.' " It seems like so little, and yet it was everything.

Where some parents felt the need to shelter their children from the knowledge of their disease the same way they might protect them from racism or sexism, I simply could not do this. First, there are some things you just cannot protect your child from, no matter what. Just as I knew I was powerless to protect Hydeia from bigotry, I knew that someday she would encounter a situation like the one in nursery school. Someday someone might reject her or hurt her because she had AIDS. The difference was that she might be old enough to understand what it meant, what it said about her. Certainly being a little black girl with AIDS was not all that Hydeia was, but I knew she'd encounter people who wouldn't look any further. From the beginning, Hydeia knew as much as she could understand about having AIDS. It was simply a fact of her life. Years later, when she spoke publicly, people sometimes remarked how matter-of-factly she said, "I have AIDS because my birth mother was an IV drug user who passed it on to me before I was born." However, if you looked at the situation and felt it important to raise a child with self-esteem, confidence, and hope, how could you handle it any other way?

The more time we spent at NIH, the clearer it became that, at least for our family, disclosure was the way. Depending on your hometown, you may or may not have met anyone else with AIDS. If you did, it would probably be someone in circumstances similar to your own, like it was with Cindy, Diana, and me. Up at NIH, though, you met mothers (along with some dads and grandparents) and kids from every background. You saw how this virus cut across all the boundaries we draw to separate ourselves from others. Rich or poor, black or white, religious or not—none of it mattered when it came to AIDS. In the eyes of whatever you choose to call the force behind the epidemic, our children were all equal, and so were we. You couldn't buy, beg, pray, or bargain your child's way out.

Once we got back from that first trip to NIH, I made it a point to get Dr. K. into the loop and to make him feel like part of the team. I knew that he had reservations about Hydeia going on protocol, and I respected his views, even if we didn't always agree. While NIH was basically managing Hydeia's care, we still needed Dr. K. at home to be involved, to cooperate with NIH, and to know what to do for Hydeia if anything happened in Las Vegas. And in those days, something was always happening.

Figuring that Dr. K. needed to see Hydeia regularly so he would know what was "normal" for her at a given point in time, I called to make an appointment. I was surprised when he said that because she was now going to NIH, he didn't think we would need him. Because he was a professional, it never occurred to me that he might have taken our going to NIH personally. "What is the problem?" I asked. "Why do you feel that we don't need you? All I'm trying to do for my daughter is see that she gets the best of both worlds—having a doctor who is really dedicated to her here and then having the benefit of world-class research up at NIH. We need someone we have confidence in, someone who can advise us when we're considering suggestions from NIH. And, Dr. K., that is who you are supposed to be."

"Okay," he said, sounding a little more comfortable. "Bring her in."

It was a typical day, with Cindy, the kids, and me running here and there, then to McDonald's for lunch before Hydeia's appointment. As we sat in Dr. K.'s waiting room, Hydeia suddenly changed. Just an hour before, she had been running around laughing. Now she slumped over on my lap, burning with fever. She was having a hard time breathing, and I could feel her fading. In the examining room, Dr. K. took one look and asked, alarmed, "How long has she been this way?"

Starting to panic, I shot back, "What the hell's in your office that made her so sick? What do you clean with?"

"Nothing," he answered. "Pat, we've got to take her to the hospital. Now!"

We practically ran to the car and drove Hydeia to the University Medical Center, where she was admitted immediately. Dr. K. followed right behind us. X rays and blood tests confirmed that she had a dangerous case of pneumonia. I phoned Dr. Pizzo at NIH, because I knew that he needed documentation on everything that happened. He also wanted Dr. K. to confirm the cause of the pneumonia through a lung biopsy or a bronch wash (a procedure in which the bronchial passages are "washed" and the wash is collected and examined to determine the presence of bacteria, viruses, fungi, and other opportunistic infectious agents). Dr. K., however, disagreed. He explained that Hydeia was in such acute distress that he wasn't comfortable with the risks either procedure involved. He wanted to give her a potent antibiotic, Bactrim, intravenously. "If we see a drastic change in the next twenty-four hours, then we'll know it's probably PCP pneumonia," he explained. "If we don't, then we may have to perform the biopsy or the wash. But I'd like to give her a chance to avoid those procedures, if we can."

Although this wasn't what Dr. Pizzo wanted, it sounded reasonable to me. Sure enough, in just a few hours Hydeia's temperature began falling, and she was breathing easier. Eighteen hours later, you could see a visible difference in her chest X rays. However, she wasn't out of the woods yet, and before she got better, she took a frightening turn for the worse. This was not something I wanted Keisha to see, because she loved Hydeia so much and, at just nine, I knew she would be frightened. I wanted to spare her that pain, if I could. At the same time, there were signs that we might be losing Hydeia. Whenever I had bad news for any of my children, I was always careful to leaven it with a ray of hope. This time, however, hope was dimming rapidly. Loren, who was always the more emotional of the two of us, was taking it hard already. How could I do this?

Desperate for guidance, I called our social worker, Lori, at NIH. After I explained why I didn't want Keisha to see her sister like that, Lori calmly said, "You need to think about Keisha's closure, if something happens to Hydeia." She was right. I tried to tell Keisha what it would be like to see Hydeia in isolation in the ICU, with all the machines surrounding her, but nothing could really prepare her. Isolation is a cold, scary place. Keisha bravely, quietly approached her sister's bed and lovingly placed her hand on Hydeia's leg.

"Don't touch me! Don't touch me!" Hydeia cried, her nerve endings hypersensitive to everything. "You hurt, you hurt!"

With a look of shock, Keisha bolted from the room crying. I followed her out into the hallway, where she stood sobbing. "Is she gonna die, Mommy? Is she gonna die?"

I hugged Keisha and gently wiped her tears with my hand. "Now, wait a minute," I said softly. "She is not dying right now. She's getting better. This is just an AIDS thing. And I promise you, Keisha, when it is time to cry, Mommy will be the first one to tell you."

Keisha dried her eyes, and after she regained her composure we went back to Hydeia's room. We could visit only for a short time, and on the way home Keisha was unusually quiet. Suddenly she said, "Mommy, if Hydeia dies, you won't want to be a mommy no more, will you?"

Keeping my eyes on the road, I tried to figure out just what she was getting at. "What do you mean?"

"It's like when people have a dog and it dies. They don't want to get another dog, because it will die, too," she reasoned. "If Hydeia dies, you won't want to be a mommy, because you don't want your other kids to die."

"I will never stop being a mommy, no matter what happens. I was your mommy before Hydeia came along, was I not? I was Kendall's, Pepe's, and Kimmie's mother before you. And I will be a mommy still, even if Hydeia dies." From that day on, I could read the look on Keisha's face that said, "Is it time yet?"

Though Hydeia's health issues affected everyone in the house, I think it was hardest of all for Keisha. As we say in this community, there are children who are infected and children who are affected—siblings primarily. AIDS certainly changed Keisha's life. The other kids were old enough to understand and independent enough not to need me as much. As smart as she was, though, Keisha was still a little girl. Keisha couldn't have asked for a father more supportive and involved than Loren. For Keisha, however, I know that didn't always make up for my frequent, unpredictable, and sometimes long absences. Try as I might to compensate for our time apart or the attention I couldn't always give, it was never enough. Looking back, I can honestly say that I did the best I could. However, the best that I could do under the circumstances was not necessarily everything that Keisha needed. I noticed that when friends and family called, it was always to see how Hydeia was doing. No one asked about Keisha, who was having a hard time, too. The exceptions were Cindy and Diana, who would make an extra effort to include her and take her places, and my best friend, Rita. But I know it wasn't the same for Keisha.

One night about a year later Keisha began complaining that her ears hurt every time she lay down. This had been going on all evening. She didn't have a temperature, and I was exhausted, but I thought it best to have it checked out, just in case. Shortly after midnight, we arrived at the emergency room. Over the next six hours doctors examined her and ran every test imaginable. Nothing. After a couple of hours in the E.R., I'd begun to suspect there was no physical problem, so I wasn't surprised. We drove home in silence as the sun rose over the desert. I was so angry that I knew if I said anything, I'd regret it. We pulled into the drive, and after I turned off the car I turned to Keisha beside me in the front seat.

"Keisha, there is nothing wrong with you," I said as she looked at me in silence. "You made Mommy sit in the hospital all night for nothing. I think I know why you did this, though. Maybe you think Mommy wouldn't take you to the hospital if something was wrong with you. But I would. If there was anything wrong with any of my kids, I would take them to the hospital. You know Hydeia goes to the hospital so much because there is something wrong with her blood. There is nothing wrong with our blood. You, me, Daddy—we don't have to go to the hospital every time we've got a little cold. But it's different for Hydeia."

Keisha said nothing, but she understood. When I was home, I tried to spend more time with her, but it wasn't always quality time. And there were moments when she made her loss painfully clear to me. A few years later Hydeia was in the hospital when Keisha graduated from sixth grade. Loren and other family members would attend, and I bought Keisha two beautiful dresses and two pairs of shoes to wear for her special day. I wanted her to know that I loved her, was proud of her, and would be thinking about her while I was away. When I got home, I found the dresses wadded up and stuffed in the bottom of her closet.

To make matters worse, Loren and I were beginning to grow apart. We made a great team when it came to dealing with the kids or meeting the challenges for Hydeia. Deep inside, however, we were each beginning to see our lives together differently. Though most of the costs of going to NIH were covered, we still had about a hundred dollars in expenses for each trip, in food, phone calls home, and miscellaneous costs. We had begun going out less, eliminating vacations, and watching our budget. When it became clear that I might have to quit working and scale back our lifestyle, we began to diverge.

Loren would do anything for Hydeia, but as we discussed the changes ahead, he could only see what we might be losing, while I always ascribed to my own mother's view: Things could always be worse. Where I saw the glass as half full, he saw it as half empty. The funny thing was, as great as we were at being there for our kids, it was becoming harder to be there for each other. Despite this, Loren and I remained together for another five years, largely because we knew the toll it would take on Hydeia and Keisha if we divorced.

One of the most difficult parts of going to NIH was the hassle of living out of a suitcase in a hotel room, with no place to cook, do laundry, or ever just feel like you were at home. Perhaps the worst part of hotel living was the feeling of being cut off from both your family at home and the other parents and families at NIH.

In June 1990 that all changed with the opening of the Children's Inn at NIH. Dr. Pizzo had long seen the need for families to have a true home away from home, and he spearheaded the effort to build this wonderful facility. Located at the northern edge of the NIH campus and a short distance from the hospital, the Children's Inn is a vast two-story, homelike facility with thirty-seven private bedroom-bathroom suites, each with two double beds, linens, television, and phone. You can do your own cooking in one of two large communal kitchen/dining room areas, take care of your laundry, make free long-distance phone calls home, and borrow everything you might need, from blow-dryers to strollers. Outdoors, the children have an incredible playground. Inside is a large, well-stocked playroom for the younger kids and a game room, complete with pool table, video games, Ping-Pong, sound system, and other amenities, for the older ones. There is a large living room, a family room (with wide-screen television and exercise machines), and a library. Open every day of the year, twenty-four hours a day, the Children's Inn serves not only the children undergoing treatment for HIV/AIDS, but those with cancer, mental illnesses, developmental disabilities, diseases of the heart, lungs, blood, and bones, growth disorders, and anything else that NIH might be researching and treating. There is no charge to stay at the inn, although you are expected to bring in your own groceries.

Staying at the Children's Inn drastically reduced some of the stress. You could pack lighter because you could do laundry there. You could eat what you wanted, when you wanted, because you had the kitchen. Small things, true. But with a child as picky and undernourished as Hydeia and many others we knew, no request for food could be delayed or ignored. You didn't have to worry about arranging for cabs to go to and from NIH every day. Most important, though, you could sit and talk with other parents, if you felt like it, and kids could play with other kids. That, I think, was one of the best things about the Children's Inn. Though you never knew exactly who you might run into when you got there, we formed a community. Especially in those early days, far too many of the children passed, as did some of their infected parents, and you never got used to that. Death is an inescapable part of living with AIDS. Children with AIDS, their siblings, and their friends usually experience more deaths before middle school than most adults will see in a lifetime.

Hydeia was always Miss Personality Plus. She made friends easily at NIH, but that meant that she lost friends, too. From one visit to the next, you never really knew who had become seriously ill or who had died. One of her first friends to pass was a beautiful little girl named Corey.

I remember Hydeia and Corey playing together, running along the top of a low wall. It was three or four months before Corey passed, and I noticed something stiff about her gait. When I asked her mother, Vicky, about it, she brushed it off with, "Oh, she's just so silly!" You didn't need to be up at NIH very long before you became attuned to the subtle early-warning signs. In Corey's case, this rigidity in her walk was an early sign of CMV, or cytomegalovirus, a herpes virus that causes mononucleosis in people with healthy immune systems. In people with HIV/AIDS, it can infect any part of the body. In Corey's case, it had attacked her eyes, resulting in blindness, and her brain.

Vicky and I had hit it off immediately. Spirited, maybe even a little wild, she was not your typical mom. She loved to party, and we passed many hours standing outside, enjoying a cigarette or talking over coffee. She loved Corey with all her heart, and I know that Corey saw the soft, maternal side that Vicky showed no one else. Like many mothers up at NIH, Vicky was also HIV-positive. She would die a few years later.

After a couple of months in which Corey's health rapidly deteriorated, Vicky decided to stop treatment at NIH and take her home, to Albany, New York, to die. "I know it's over," she told me softly one day. "I know the fight is over." The next time I heard from Vicky, Corey had passed. Telling Hydeia about anyone's death was, for me, always a delicate situation. Rarely did I tell her the minute I got the news. Usually I would wait for the right moment, or wait for her to ask how someone was doing or when we were going to see them again. I wanted Hydeia to understand, but I didn't want her to be afraid. In Corey's case, Hydeia could see for herself how her friend went from wearing glasses to being blind, from walking with difficulty to not walking at all. When it was clear that Corey was not going to get better, I said to Hydeia, "I think that Corey might be going to heaven soon. I think God wants to bring her home so that she can dance and play and sing again, and see."

Hydeia's face brightened a bit when she said, "Oh! So when Corey dies, she won't be sick anymore?"

"That's right. She won't be sick anymore. She'll be just like we knew her—dancing and playing with all the kids in heaven."

That seemed to satisfy Hydeia, but she was a bright, curious child, and one day she remarked, "You know, Mommy, if I die, there won't be any room in heaven for me."

I knew what she meant: Heaven was already full of children who had died of AIDS. But what could I say? Without thinking, I answered, "Well, as long as there isn't any room in heaven for you, God won't bring you home."

When the subject arose, I tried to keep it casual. I didn't want to scare her, and to be honest, I didn't want to talk about it. Here again, you could say that Hydeia was beyond her years. At least she was a few steps ahead of her mother.

Not long after this talk, Hydeia befriended a little girl named Alexandria, who was about three or four (because so many of the children were so small for their age, you couldn't always tell how old they were), and Alexandria's two sisters. When it was clear that time was growing short, the sisters came down to Hydeia's room and one of them said, "Alexandria is dying. Do you want to come up and say good-bye?"

Hydeia didn't answer, but once they had left, she turned to me and said, "Mommy, I want to go say good-bye to Alexandria and let her know that she's going to be okay."

For once, I was at a loss for words. It's not as if I hadn't given it any thought; I had. Because I did not want to stand at a baby's deathbed, because I knew one day I might be standing next to Hydeia's and truly felt that once would be enough, I said no. Of course, I couldn't just say no outright. I had to have my reasons. My mind raced as Hydeia said, "Mommy? I really want to go and say good-bye to her."

Trying my hardest to disguise my personal feelings, I put on my calm, reasonable mommy voice. "Hydeia, if Mommy was real sick, and you, Daddy, and Keisha had your last moments with me, would you want to have a whole bunch of other people there? Or would you like to be with me by yourself, so we could say good-bye to each other and have time together?"

She thought for a moment and said, "No. I wouldn't want your time to be spent with other people. I would want to be with you."

"Well, I think that's probably how Alexandria's mommy and daddy feel. They want this to be a family time and to spend the time with Alexandria themselves."

"Oh, okay," she said softly.

"So I don't think it would be a good idea, do you?"

"Oh, no," she said.

I breathed a silent sigh of relief. My reactions were shaped by the experiences of another little girl: me. When I was seven, my father had died suddenly of a heart attack due to high blood pressure. The youngest of seven and the child of a loving but stoic mother, I was protected in a way. Of course, I loved and would miss my father, a hardworking, generous man, but I was too young to understand death. Daddy was asleep, they reassured me. He was going to heaven. As always, my mother faced this loss with her usual strength. I know she loved my father, and I'm sure it was one of the most difficult times of her life, but whatever tears she cried, she cried alone. There were no dramatic, emotional outbursts, no moment when my mother was not in complete control.

A few weeks after my father's funeral, I was home with my mother when she opened a large envelope that came in the mail. She gasped as she took out an eight-by-ten black-and-white photograph of my father lying in his coffin. "Oh no," she said in a steady voice. "I don't want this." She lit the four corners of the picture, and as flames engulfed my father's image, I asked, "Why are you burning it?"

"We don't want to remember him in his casket," she said simply. "We want to remember him alive—fishing and happy."

"Oh," I said, though I thought burning Daddy's picture was mean of her. I had seen him in the casket, so what was so strange about having a picture of that? Looking back, I could see that was how my mother protected us. Now I was trying to protect Hydeia, but her experience of death was so different from my own.

A few hours later Alexandria's sisters reappeared. "Hydeia, my mom said if you want to say good-bye to Alexandria, you need to come now," one of them said quickly.

Hydeia looked at me, and before I could open my mouth she said, "Mommy, they *want* me to come and say good-bye. We need to go."

I glanced at Dr. Brigitta Mueller, one of the doctors caring for Hydeia who happened to be in the room, with a look that said, "I can't do this." She got it and offered to take Hydeia herself. I could have let her, but that would have been too easy. Maybe it was my turn to learn. "Okay," I said. "Come on, Hydeia. Let's go."

At the door to Alexandria's room, I paused and drew a deep breath. In all the time I'd known Alexandria's mother, she always seemed to be falling apart and crying over everything. Though I liked her, I have to admit that I sometimes had a hard time with her emotional intensity. In fact, one reason I'd tried to convince Hydeia not to come was that I expected to find Alexandria's mother overwrought.

I knocked softly, and once inside, Hydeia walked right up to Alexandria's bedside and held her friend's tiny hand. Soft gospel music filled the room. Alexandria's mother, father, and sisters were there at the bedside. A scene that first struck me as eerie revealed itself as a beautiful closing to a precious life. Alexandria's mother exuded peace and acceptance. She was a better woman than I feared I could be. For all of her troubles, God had granted her the grace to recognize when the fight was done and the freedom from anguish to go with her child through these last days in love, not fear.

"Alexandria, don't worry," I heard Hydeia say quietly. "God will be waiting for you, and you'll be able to sing and dance." *Who is this child?* I remember thinking of Hydeia.

We didn't stay long. After Alexandria passed that evening, Hydeia asked, "Mommy, when I die, are you going to come to my funeral?"

"What makes you think I'm not going to die before you?" I asked, desperately applying some mom psychology. "I'm older, you know."

"Mommy, kids with AIDS are dying all the time," she said matter-of-factly.

"Yeah, but there's a good possibility that I will die first. So will you come to my funeral?"

"Yeah!"

"Okay, so let's make a deal: If I die first, you will be at my funeral. If you die first, Mommy will be at your funeral."

A big hug sealed our deal.

A day or so later, against my own instincts, I agreed to attend Alexandria's memorial service in the fourteenth-floor chapel of the NIH hospital. I quietly took a seat at the back of the room, near Lori. I was fine until Alexandria's parents and sisters entered pushing the baby's empty stroller. I remember they had her quilt inside and a doll that she always had with her. "I can't do this," I whispered to Lori. I knew that if I stayed, my grief and my fear would incapacitate me. No matter what anyone else would have liked of me, my daughter needed me more. I couldn't afford to lose it emotionally, because I feared that if I ever let go, I'd never recover. I quietly rose and left.

FOUR

*D*espite everything, Hydeia retained her outgoing, bubbly personality. Though small for her age and frail, she was always outgoing, outspoken, and sometimes even a little outrageous. She sang whenever the mood struck her—usually little songs she made up spontaneously—without a trace of self-consciousness. She liked dressing up, putting on makeup (I'd buy bags of the cheap stuff for her to play with during long hospital days), and acting cute. Though very much a little girl, from as early as age five Hydeia seemed older than her years. If she had something to say, or if she felt that something was wrong, she let you know it. Lurking under that soft, little-girl voice, the impeccable manners, and those big brown eyes were a will of steel and a strong sense of justice. It was only natural that she grew into the activist she is today.

During those first couple of years at NIH, I devoted countless hours to public speaking to raise awareness about pediatric AIDS and gather support for Reach Out. Often Cindy, Diana, and I would bring Hydeia along. She would sit either on the stage or right down in front, listening attentively as I told my

story and explained our dream for Reach Out. I always introduced Hydeia (and Hydeia also spoke with other people, including Cindy) because I wanted people to see the face of AIDS.
I wanted them to realize that this crisis was not about where it
came from, how you got it, and who was getting it but about the
real, living children who had it—children like Hydeia. I also
wanted to show people—and Hydeia—that AIDS was nothing
to be ashamed of. In those days most people's concept of AIDS
came from the media. The prevailing image of a pediatric AIDS
child was either someone discriminated against or ostracized or
someone living in secret terror to avoid being discriminated
against or ostracized. Hydeia was bright and attentive, but it
surprised me the first few times she politely interrupted me to
say, "Mommy, you forgot to tell them about . . ."

Though we talked about her having AIDS and dealt with it
every day, she revealed many of her deepest feelings through
play. Every so often, she would pretend to be April O'Neil, rov-
ing reporter and friend of the popular Teenage Mutant Ninja
Turtles. Sometimes she would say, "Mommy, let's play April
O'Neil"; other times she would slip into character spontaneously. One early exchange went something like this:

"Mrs. Broadbent, do you have a daughter with AIDS?"

"Yes," I said.

"Are you mad?"

"Mad about what?"

"Mad because you always have to be in the hospital and away
from Keisha and be away from home?"

"Of course I'm not mad," I replied. "I'm happy to be with my
daughter."

After a moment she broke character to ask, "Mommy, when I
die, are you going to come to my funeral?"

Hydeia played April O'Neil with everyone, including other
children at the Children's Inn and Lori Wiener. "My name is
April O'Neil, and I'm here at NIH and I'm going to talk to Lori

I love my mommy. Corey is in Heaven. We can always remember our friends who are in Heaven. They are standing by us. We can remember them. I think I will go to Heaven too when I get old. When I get there, Corey and Ezra and Blayne and other children I once knew will be there for me to play with.

The end.

Love, Hydeia
Age eight

about kids having AIDS. What do you think about kids having AIDS?"

"I don't know," Lori answered. "What do you think?"

"Kids are dying, and doctors have to do something," "April" replied.

Lori decided to make a video showing children with AIDS discussing their thoughts and feelings. Entitled *I Need a Friend*, it featured Hydeia, a little girl named Tanya, and a slightly older boy named Joey DiPaolo. Joey, from Staten Island, New York, was infected at age four through a blood transfusion during heart surgery. I'm happy to report that as of this writing both Tanya and Joey are still with us today, and Joey is also a leading AIDS activist; over the years he and Hydeia have shared the stage on many occasions.

For most of the film Hydeia—skinny as a rail, with braided pigtails and a no-nonsense demeanor—holds a microphone and "interviews" the other two about having HIV/AIDS. In several brief segments, she sings her own compositions with such titles as "The Hospital Song" ("I go to the hospital, I need a friend, I have AIDS") and "The Teasing Song" ("I walk away from them. . . . I think some people have to learn their lesson"). These were not perfectly rhymed, verse-chorus-verse masterpieces, but you got the point. Through it all, Hydeia and the other two are surprisingly nonchalant about living with AIDS. When Hydeia asks Tanya and Joey if they know that they could die from AIDS, they say yes, but they make it clear that the most important thing is having friends now. (Part of the film shows Hydeia and me a year or so before, talking about the day the teacher sprayed bleach in her face.)

Around this time, Elizabeth Glaser, whose daughter, Ariel, had been treated by Dr. Pizzo prior to her death and whose son, Jake, eventually went on protocol, was working through the Pediatric AIDS Foundation to jump-start research and create awareness and acceptance of children with HIV. Lori and Dr.

Pizzo showed Elizabeth a videotape of Hydeia. She was so impressed that she left a gift for Hydeia, a video shot at one of the foundation's first major fund-raisers, featuring stars such as Whoopi Goldberg and Rhea Perlman singing nursery rhymes. Hydeia enjoyed the video, but to me it meant even more, because Elizabeth was probably the single person most responsible for saving Hydeia's life. Through her intensive, relentless lobbying of politicians, researchers, and government health officials, she was instrumental in obtaining funding for the pediatric AIDS protocols. Without Elizabeth's compassion and commitment, Hydeia would not be here today. Although Hydeia would not meet Elizabeth for another year or so, she was already an important part of our lives.

Back in Las Vegas, Diana, Cindy, and I were working hard to make Reach Out a reality. With my background in social work and Diana's as a teacher and administrator, we knew about the ins and outs of fund-raising and growing an organization from the ground up. Still, we could be happily surprised and bitterly disappointed by the twists and turns in the road to creating the haven we envisioned. Initially, we had thought in terms of a day-care facility, but county laws prohibited licensed facilities from accepting children who were ill. Since we could expect most of our clients to be ill or running fevers, we had to apply instead as a learning center. The difference was partly technical, but it also meant that we had a broader mission. In addition to providing day care for infected children and their affected siblings from infancy through age twelve, we also provided support groups for parents and siblings, informational programs, and assistance through a cooperative, where families could pick up good used clothing and other necessities. We had volunteers who would go with parents to the hospital and help them however they could.

Money was hard to come by, and finding a facility was nearly impossible. Fortunately, a local church offered to lease us a house it owned for an annual fee of one dollar. We then turned to the community and cajoled, begged, and persuaded to obtain everything we needed to open our doors: new cribs, playpens, changing tables, extra clothing, medical supplies, linens, strollers, a commercial dishwasher, tables, chairs, toys, beds. We enlisted parents to help with routine cleanup and maintenance. We convinced the local K mart to give us disposable diapers that had minor damage to the outside packaging (they couldn't sell them in that condition) and local organizations to give us a discount on baby formula. We set to work getting builders, contractors, plumbers, painters, and other professionals to donate their services for the extensive cleanup and renovation work.

Despite all this generosity, we always needed more, so Diana, Cindy, and I just kept on talking. Now, though, Hydeia often had an "official" spot on the program. We never really prepared her remarks ahead of time, and no one told Hydeia what to say. I never knew what to expect. While she always delivered essentially the same message, she would change things about her presentation depending on how she felt. Somehow, though, even at that tender age, she had a way of talking to people that really touched them. I guess part of it was the fact that she was not uncomfortable about having AIDS. She wasn't up there asking people for their pity, she wanted only their understanding and support. She didn't ask people to treat her differently, only like any other child.

It was comforting to know that at NIH Hydeia was getting the best care in the world. Still, her health had not improved significantly, even with the intravenous CD4 and the oral ddI. After a few months on protocol, Hydeia was not one bit better. If anything, she was precisely where she had been before we came to NIH. It was baffling. All the other kids I saw on protocol seemed to be less sick, and less often, yet Hydeia continued failing.

Dr. Pizzo reassured me that all the children on protocol were getting the actual meds; in other words, no one received a placebo or sugar water. "Well, Dr. Pizzo, if that's the case," I answered, "I find it hard to believe that everyone else seems to be doing pretty well on ddI, and Hydeia is still getting sick."

"I know," he said. "But just because your horse is lagging behind, you're not going to give up. You don't know. That horse may have the potential to gain and to win. We have to give the drugs a chance to prove themselves."

"I understand that, Dr. Pizzo. But this is how I see it: If my horse is behind, then he's down on his knees, common sense would tell me it's time to get off and walk him back to the stables before he drops dead."

Dr. Pizzo laughed in spite of himself; he agreed. It was possible, he said, that Hydeia could not absorb the ddI in the oral form because of her stomach problems. "What if we do it IV?" he suggested, and offered to arrange for compassionate assignment, so that Hydeia could get intravenous ddI. ("Compassionate-assignment" policy allows patients to obtain medications that have not yet been approved for use in their population if there is reason to believe that they might benefit. I believe that Hydeia was one of the first, if not the first, child to receive IV ddI.) Because ddI had just been approved in 1989 and was not yet widely used in children, no one knew exactly what we could expect. AZT and ddI were the "miracle" drugs of their time, but both came with a long list of potentially serious side effects: damage to white blood cells, the heart, and nerves; seizures; and liver failure; in addition to the more mundane headaches, light-headedness, dizziness, and difficulty concentrating, eating, and sleeping. Between the two, however, ddI was considered less toxic than AZT. From the short time we had been going to NIH, I had seen enough to convince me that for Hydeia, at that point, AZT would be a last resort.

"If we give Hydeia the IV ddI, would you be willing to keep her on the protocol?" Dr. Pizzo asked. Knowing that this might be Hydeia's only hope, I said yes.

Fortunately, Hydeia tolerated IV ddI remarkably well. You couldn't exactly say she was getting better, but she wasn't getting worse, and with AIDS that is a major accomplishment. The staff at NIH and Hydeia's doctors at home seemed to have a handle on most of her chronic problems—the sinusitis, the lymphoid interstitial pneumonia, and whatever bizarre opportunistic infection happened to catch on. Though it was no laughing matter, it became something of a running joke with the doctors, who came to know Hydeia as the patient whose penchant for picking up exotic viruses, germs, and fungi sent them running to their textbooks. Nocardia, pseudomonas, alternaria, aspergillus—they reminded me of odd names for strange little girls. In reality, they were omnipresent potential killers. For many, information and treatment were scant; even the NIH doctors would confess these were infections they might have heard about in med school but had never seen or treated before. Some were invaders rarely if ever seen in humans before AIDS "opened the door" for them, so to speak. For example, for alternaria—a fungus rare in humans that can attack the brain—doctors had to track down the only existing cache of medicine, which was in London. To attack aspergillus, another fungus, doctors prescribed amphotericin B, an antifungal drug known among the medical cognoscenti as "shake and bake" because it caused high fevers and chills so intense even someone as small as Hydeia could make a steel hospital bed shake. Every time Hydeia was on shake and bake, it made her so sick she couldn't leave her room.

The problem that seemed the least urgent from a medical perspective but that weighed on us most was Hydeia's nutritional status. She was still picking at her food, no matter how we catered to her. You couldn't even pay her to eat. I remember Cindy saying, "If you eat some soup, I'll give you a dollar," and Hydeia answering, "I don't want a dollar." For Hydeia, "eating soup" meant licking off the few drops that clung to the spoon. She would gingerly lick the butter off bread but never take a bite. She liked French fries, though her idea of eating them in-

volved breaking a single fry in half and squeezing out and eating
the soft white potato center. One fry, two fries, and she was
done. In her entire life, I'd never once heard Hydeia say, "I'm
hungry." My frustration and fear over her not eating was so intense I could barely sit at the table with her. Our daily routine revolved around spending about two hours at breakfast, two at
lunch, and two at dinner trying to get her to eat something. An
hour or two after we'd finished with one meal, it was time to
start all over again. I got so tired of talking, pleading, cajoling,
and bargaining with her to eat that I was down to a hundred
pounds and subsisting on milk and Ensure.

At NIH we met a kind, understanding doctor from Africa
named Sam Adeni-Jones. He brought fresh enthusiasm to the
challenge of getting her to eat. Despite my long descriptions of
Hydeia's eating problems, he wanted to do things formally, so he
asked me to keep a chart of everything she ate. When I showed
it to him, he exclaimed, "My God, she hardly eats anything!"

"Hello?" I replied, a little shortly, I'm sure. "I think I told you
that." When he recommended that she should be drinking six
cans of Ensure a day, I just looked at him. "I can't even get her
to drink water unless it's in an ice cube she can chew," I said.
"How am I going to get six cans of Ensure into her?"

Dr. Adeni seemed skeptical. "I just don't believe she's that bad
about eating," he said.

"Oh, you don't?" I said. "Then I'll tell you what. It's two
o'clock and she hasn't had lunch yet. Why don't you do me a
favor? You take her down to the cafeteria and you feed her."

"Okay," he said, smiling as if this was going to be a piece of
cake. Two hours later he was back. "Can I talk to you?" he
asked wearily.

"So what happened?" I asked.

"She took a French fry, and—"

"And she broke it half and squeezed it, right?"

"How did you know?" he asked.

"What do you think I've been trying to tell you?"

"I gave her ice cream—all kids like ice cream. I got her a hamburger, the fries. Nothing worked." He looked stunned.

It was then that we decided to put Hydeia on total parenteral nutrition, also known as TPN. Every night, from 9 P.M. to 9 A.M. Hydeia received a special mixture of carbohydrates, protein, fat, vitamins, water, electrolytes, and minerals through her Hickman. While TPN proved a godsend for her, medically speaking, it was yet one more aspect of her care that required constant monitoring. Like anything else introduced through the Hickman, TPN carried additional risks of infection, embolism, and irritation of her vessels, in addition to heart problems, electrolyte imbalances, dehydration, and hyperglycemia, among other things. Traditionally, TPN is a temporary measure, for patients who have suffered severe trauma or disease in the digestive system, who are in a coma or are otherwise unable to digest food normally. Hydeia, however, would be on TPN for about a year and a half without any major complications. We knew we had made the right decision, because Hydeia slowly began gaining weight, from the twenty-seven pounds she weighed when we began to about fifty-eight pounds when we stopped. (Over the first few weeks off TPN, she lost some excess fluid to stabilize between forty-nine and fifty-two pounds.)

In addition to the stress and worry that came standard-issue with having a chronically, potentially terminally ill child, there were some basic parenting issues. In the fall of 1990, health issues drove our decision to remove Hydeia from school. She needed the extra rest and couldn't risk picking up a common but potentially serious infection from another student. On top of that, for those first five years at NIH, the seemingly never-ending stream of problems, hospital admissions, and last-minute flights to Bethesda would have left a regular school program in shambles. Under the federal Individuals with Disabilities Education Act, Hydeia, like every child in America with a physical, psychiatric, emotional, or learning disability, was entitled to a free appropriate public education tailored to suit her unique needs. For us that meant home tutoring, and in the beginning, I wasn't that concerned about either the quantity or the quality of the education our local school district provided. To be honest—painfully honest—for all the hope I held for my daughter, I had no rational reason to believe that she would live long enough for education to matter.

I, like most moms I came to know at NIH, felt overwhelmed, despite the excellent support services offered us. Sure, we could commiserate with one another, participate in an organized support group, or, in my case, turn to Lori Wiener or my good friend Rita for a solid shoulder and a sympathetic ear. However, these were small rays of light against the towering shadow AIDS cast over everything. Nothing was our own—not our time, our thoughts, our attention, sometimes not even our feelings. AIDS wrote the schedule, AIDS spelled out the itinerary, AIDS ruled our lives.

Even away from home, we continued running households out of suitcases. The Children's Inn and the hospital at NIH were both wonderful places, but the work of being a mom never stopped in either place. Children's Inn was a home away from home in every sense of the word, which meant that moms were still shopping, cooking, cleaning, bathing, doing laundry, ironing, and making beds, in addition to being full-time amateur nurses. When children were hospitalized at NIH for any period, parents usually stayed in the room with their child, sleeping on a cot, washing, dressing, and basically living there for however long the stay. We were expected to provide all of the nonmedical care patients usually look to nurses and other hospital staff to provide: fetching water and food, changing the sheets and making the bed, washing and feeding, and alerting the nurses and doctors if something looked suspicious. There were times when Hydeia and I remained together in the same room for a month or more at a stretch, without any break beyond the few minutes here and there when I could sneak out to have a cigarette or grab a cup of coffee.

It was a strange, difficult, and highly abnormal situation. I loved Hydeia and I loved being with her, but there were times when we both could have used a break from each other. Being cooped up together 24/7 for weeks on end was no picnic. I remember playing hide-and-seek with Hydeia in the room. That might sound impossible, but she was still so small, she could fit in places you wouldn't even notice. I would lie on the bed, cover my eyes, and count while Hydeia hid. Then I'd quietly open a book and start reading. Every couple of pages, I'd say, "Oh, I guess she's not under the bed. I wonder where she could be. . . ." Then I'd read a couple more pages. "Not in the bathroom . . ." all the while never getting up off the bed. "You're hiding really good, Hydeia, wherever you are!" I'd call out brightly. A couple more pages.

I admit, I felt terrible when I did it, but I don't think anyone who has lived this would begrudge me these stolen moments. Certainly, anyone who knew me up at NIH realized I needed them—along with the psychiatrist Lori arranged for me to see and the sleeping pills he prescribed. Overall, for Hydeia's sake, I held it together, but at a price. If I ever lost it, it wasn't in tears but in anger. And even that I managed to rein in most of the time, because I knew I couldn't afford to let the situation beat me down. I had seen other parents who simply could not handle the isolation and stress of long hospital stays and never came back to NIH. That was not an option for us, so I just kept going, like some bionic woman with a big Energizer battery on her back, going and going and going. Did I lose it sometimes? Sure.

For these years, except for Loren and a handful of other people, such as Diana and Cindy, I didn't talk much about what was happening. It wasn't that I deliberately shut people out, although some did feel that way. For me, living it was just about all I could manage. To spend hours and hours on the phone every day—time I did not have—replaying the tape was almost worse. It meant that a bad day or a frightening conversation never ended. Instead of riding the roller coaster once, it was like spinning and looping over and over again, with no escape. At least as long as I kept things to myself or shared them with only those familiar with the tests, the infections, the procedures, the medications—the reality—hope remained in my grasp. Telling and retelling the latest episode—and some days there were a dozen episodes—not only drained me emotionally but exposed me to everyone else's fears and sadness. Even when people were saying the "right" things, they were the wrong things. People couldn't help but have questions, but every question rang in my ears like doubt. Nothing could shake my fragile confidence like the well-intentioned "What if the new antibiotic doesn't work?" or "What will you do if Hydeia has to go back into the hospital?" or even a simple "What does the doctor think?" I had a hard enough time answering these questions for myself. I couldn't do it for everyone else.

My best friend, Rita, had moved to San Diego by then. Though we didn't see each other that often, we had the kind of relationship where we could go a month without talking and pick up like we'd just seen each other yesterday. She is Keisha's godmother, and I remember how happy she was for us when we adopted Hydeia. For a while after Hydeia was diagnosed, I called her frequently and told her what was going on. I knew there was nothing Rita would not do for me. Every time we talked, though, she would cry, then I would cry, and by the time we hung up, I was an emotional wreck. Gradually, I stopped calling. During a visit to Las Vegas, Rita confronted me. I was taken aback; why I couldn't call seemed so obvious to me. "It takes every ounce of control I have just to keep myself level so I can think and do what I need to do without getting emotional," I told Rita. "When I talk to you, it's too much for me, emotionally."

"You don't get it," she said. "I'm sitting here, and I see everything you and your family are going through. I see your suffering, and you have to understand what I'm going through."

Odd as it sounds, I'd never thought about Hydeia's situation in terms of how other people saw it. I knew family and friends cared about us, of course, but I'd never seen their pain. For me, it was all about getting through, not one day at a time but sometimes one minute at a time. Unlike my friends and family, I didn't worry about me. I couldn't afford to.

Not long after we started going to NIH, Loren agreed that I would call him and then he could share the most important news with my mother, my siblings, and a few close friends. I called him just about every day and kept him posted. Sometimes, when things were not going well, Loren would try to comfort me by telling me it was going to be all right. "But," I would reply, "you're not here. You haven't seen the parents at the deathbeds, or witnessed what came before that or after. You don't look at Hydeia through the same eyes I do, silently running down a mental checklist of every little symptom, every little sign, every little hint that we might lose her this time."

Ironically, the night we almost lost Hydeia, there was no sign. At this point we were going to NIH about every three weeks and staying about two days, if all ran smoothly. Having a low-grade fever had become normal for Hydeia. Sometimes, though, her temperature would suddenly shoot up dangerously high. Dr. K. had talked with Dr. Pizzo about this, but the phenomenon had never occurred at NIH. When Hydeia ran a slight fever right before we were leaving to catch our flight home, Dr. Pizzo recommended she be admitted overnight so he could study the strange temperature spikes. I agreed, though I told him that I'd seen dozens of these fevers, and this didn't look like one of them. It had been lingering at 101 degrees for a while, and that wasn't the usual pattern. Still, because these spikes might have indicated a serious bacterial infection known as MAI (mycobacterium avium-intracellulare, sometimes called MAC), which causes fever, night sweats, wasting (extreme and rapid weight loss), and diarrhea, we stayed. NIH could make a definitive diagnosis if they could culture her blood during fever, when the bacteria level was highest.

That whole day Hydeia had been up, running around and playing at the hospital. I had monitored her closely, and her temperature held at a steady 101.1, then up a little to 101.2. Around seven-thirty that evening I had put her to bed, intending to leave early the next morning for home. We were sharing the room with another little girl who had AIDS, Tamara, and her grandmother. I lay down on my cot, and Hydeia and I were talking back and forth a little, about nothing in particular, when her words stopped making sense.

Thinking she was playing, I asked, "What are you talking about?"

She sat up suddenly and said, "My head hurts, Mommy. My head hurts."

I jumped up and touched her forehead. She felt a little warm, so I took her temperature with a hospital thermometer, which was in Celsius. I knew 37 Celsius was a normal 98.6 Fahrenheit, so this 39 was somewhere around 102. I walked quickly down to the nurses' station and said, "I think Hydeia's fever is trying to spike." The nurse I spoke with assured me she would keep an eye on it but didn't seem alarmed. I hurried back to the room, where Hydeia's whole appearance had begun to change. Her color was off, and her expression was strange. I took her temperature again. It took only ten minutes for it to surge to 39, or 103. I went to the nurse and told her. She promised to come right in. By the time I got to the room, though, Hydeia was going down fast. Sitting on the side of the bed, I could feel her shaking. Within ten minutes her fever had climbed to 105.8 Fahrenheit.

This time I ran. "Her temp is over forty-one!" I screamed at the nurse. "You need to come now!"

"I'll be there in a minute. I'm doing something," she replied.

"No! You will come *now*!"

The nurse could barely keep up with me; I was running. When she could not get a blood-pressure reading, a look of alarm swept across her face and she said urgently, "I need to get Dr. Anderson." On her way out, she called to another nurse to get him, stat. Meanwhile, I could see Hydeia fading away, as the tremors became so violent her bed shook. About the time Dr. Anderson arrived, Hydeia's eyes had rolled up back into her head, and I heard someone ask Tamara and her grandmother to please leave the room. Usually they just closed the curtain between the beds, so I knew this was serious. Dr. Anderson called for Dr. Pizzo, and within seconds, it seemed, they were pumping meds into her Hickman like you would put gas into a car.

Everything about the scene was both unreal and too real. I had the sense to remain calm and step back, because I knew that if I got too emotional, I'd be asked to wait outside. So I sank down onto the cot, where all I could see were the backs of the doctors and nurses surrounding her bed. At one point Dr. Anderson came over and started saying something about her fever being so high and her blood pressure being so low, but it was like there was a fog between us. I couldn't really understand what he meant. Then the sound of a voice over the hospital public-address system broke through: "Code blue, thirteen west, room three-fifty-seven, bed A! Code blue, thirteen west, room three-fifty-seven, bed A!" It took a few seconds to realize that they were talking about Hydeia, and that she was dying.

Suddenly a new team of doctors rushed in, the crash team.

Though from where I sat on the cot, I shouldn't have been able to see what they were doing, I did. It was as if I were floating directly above Hydeia and could see everything. Her eyes were closed and her body was shaking. I saw them cut into her wrist to insert an internal blood-pressure monitor. I saw them injecting the meds, and I saw the tense, worried glances they exchanged. Time stood still as I watched my daughter die.

An eternity passed in twenty minutes or so. Half an hour later Hydeia was still unconscious but stable enough to be transferred down to the intensive care unit on the tenth floor. Someone explained to me that I couldn't go down with her now, but they would let me know as soon as I could see her, probably in twenty minutes or so. I nodded, the whole time thinking, *Now it's Hydeia's turn to go.* I knew I had to call Loren, but I don't remember exactly when I did that.

In ICU Hydeia lay quietly—too quietly—surrounded by machines in a sort of cubbyhole. Only the beeps and hums of the various monitors or the occasional soft-spoken word broke the heavy silence. Every patient had a round-the-clock nurse. I sank into the chair at the head of Hydeia's bed and looked at my baby. Soon an ICU doctor was there, explaining in a calm, deliberate way that Hydeia was critical but stable. However, he warned gently, no one could predict if she would ever wake up or when. And if she did wake up, there was no telling how she would be. She might not be able to walk, talk, think, or do anything on her own, he warned me. "She might not know who you are," he added. I nodded that I understood, but I did not.

ICU visits are limited to fifteen minutes, and when it was time, the doctor urged me to go back to the inn and get some rest.

"I don't want to leave her," I said.

"Yes, I understand. But you look exhausted, Mrs. Broadbent. We don't want you to get sick."

It took a minute for that to register. Then it hit me. Because I was black and because my daughter had AIDS, he just assumed

Hydeia at eighteen months.

Just a regular kid at a Las Vegas park at age four, shortly after being diagnosed with HIV.

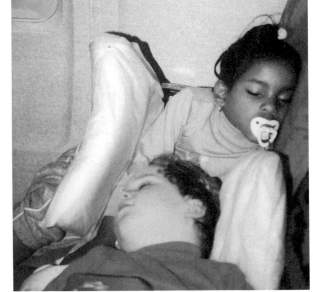

Hydeia and her best friend, Tyler, on their first trip to the National Institutes of Health in 1989.

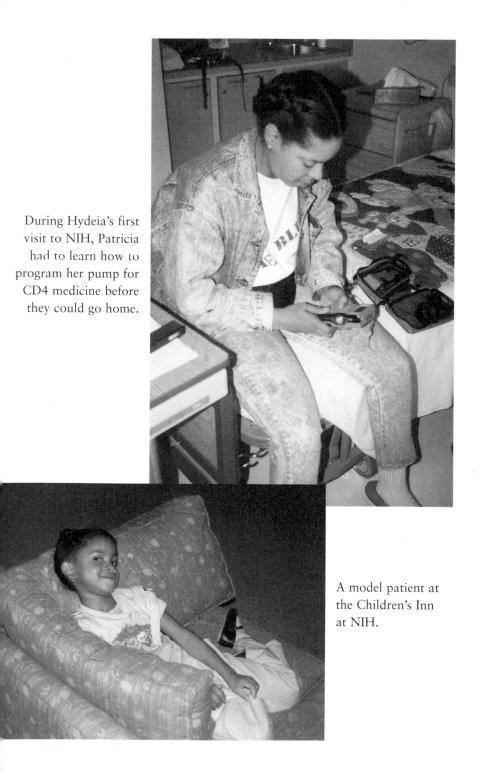

During Hydeia's first visit to NIH, Patricia had to learn how to program her pump for CD4 medicine before they could go home.

A model patient at the Children's Inn at NIH.

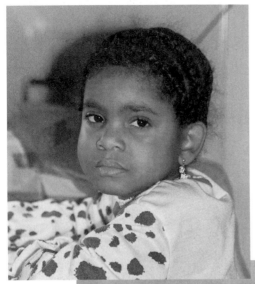

Hydeia shortly after lung surgery in 1991.

Hydeia's half brother, Mikey, and Tyler.

Janet Jackson visiting Hydeia on her ninth birthday.

Seven-year-old Hydeia at the Pediatric AIDS Foundation's Time for Heroes picnic in 1991. *From left:* Susie Zeegan, Susan DeLaurentis, and Elizabeth Glaser.

At the Time for
Heroes picnic in 1992,
Elizabeth Glaser talks
about her admiration
for Hydeia.

Hydeia and her sister Keisha (*sitting*), on the set of *Sister Act* with
Pat (*standing left*), Whoopi Goldberg, and Harvey Keitel.

Rachel Davis and Hydeia after the taping of
"A Conversation with Magic" for
Nickelodeon in 1991.

Hydeia and baby Patricia (Trisha) preparing to leave
for the Children's Inn in 1992.

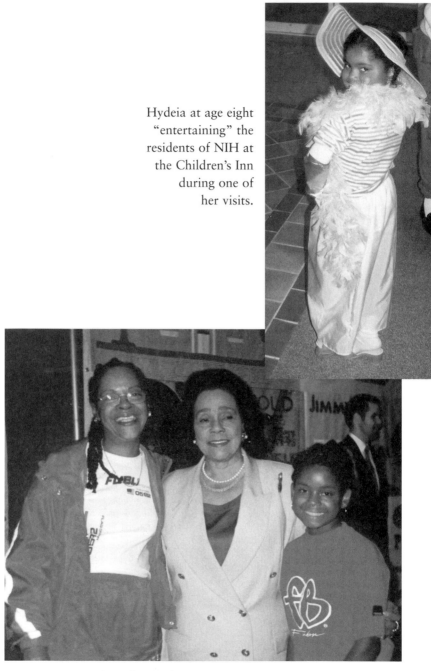

Hydeia at age eight "entertaining" the residents of NIH at the Children's Inn during one of her visits.

Pat and Hydeia with Coretta Scott King (*center*) at Clark Atlanta University in 1999 to view the NAMES Project Foundation AIDS Memorial Quilt.

Hydeia in 1994, onstage with
one of her favorite singers,
Engelbert Humperdinck.

Hydeia and Maury Povich, after she made an appearance on
a special Christmas episode of his talk show in 1992.

Hydeia speaking at Think Life's annual awards banquet in 1993.

Hydeia sings with Billy Ray Cyrus at the Grand Ole Opry in Nashville in 1993. *(Courtesy of Mary Jane Kilgore)*

Hydeia speaks at a public school in
Montgomery, Alabama, in 1994.

Brock Peters, Hydeia, Angela Bassett, and Frank Holoman at the
Black Achievers Awards ceremony in 1994.

In 1995, Hydeia received recognition for her work during the J. E. Abernathy Community Outreach, Inc., first annual awards luncheon, "Putting Faces on AIDS." Attending were (*standing*) Keisha and Delores Bullard, president and executive director of the Hydeia L. Broadbent Foundation, and (*sitting*) Hydeia, Trisha, and Pat.

Hydeia, at age eleven, with a group of children who wanted to meet her after one of her speaking engagements.

Hydeia with First Lady
Hillary Clinton in 1997.

Dr. Jerry Case, of the
National Conference for
Community and Justice,
presents Hydeia with the
Community Hero Award
in 1998 in Las Vegas.

Hydeia accepting her 1999 Essence Award, which was
given to her in recognition of her work on
behalf of AIDS awareness.
(Courtesy of Essence *magazine;*
Richard E. Allen, photographer)

Hydeia's proud parents, Loren (*right*) and Pat (*center*), at the
Essence Awards in 1999. Also with them is Conrad Bullard.

At the Essence Jazz Festival in New Orleans in 1999. *From left:* Rohan Marley, Lauryn Hill, Hydeia, Patti LaBelle, Pat, and Deborah Langford, former vice president of *Essence*.

Hydeia (*front*) with her family and the staff of the Hydeia L. Broadbent Foundation after she received the Humanitarian Award from the American Red Cross in 1999. *From left:* R. Cassandra Sheard, Kendall (Hydeia's brother), Pat, Delores Bullard, Conrad Bullard, and Mary Franklin (Kendall's wife).

Hydeia at her sixteenth birthday party.

Pat with all of her children at Hydeia's sixteenth birthday party. *Front row from left:* Trisha, Hydeia. *Middle:* Pat, Paige, Keisha, Kim. *Back:* Kendall.

that I must have it, too. "I am not infected!" I replied sharply. "Don't worry about me getting sick. I can hang."

"Oh, oh, okay," he said sheepishly. "It's just—"

I cut him off with a glare, then turned toward the waiting room. I had been advised to call Loren and tell him to fly east. I wanted him there, of course, but I also knew that his presence was another sign that this might be the end, that Hydeia's chances for meaningful recovery appeared very slim. Before I called him, though, I wanted to get myself under control. I got some coffee in the cafeteria, stepped outside, and lit a cigarette. I was shaking so hard, I couldn't even smoke it. Wave upon wave of grief crashed over me. Every time I dried my eyes and pulled myself together enough to call home, I got pulled down again in an undertow of tears. *I've got to stop,* I told myself. It wasn't just all about control and appearances, either. I knew that sometime in the next few hours or days, I might confront a critical, life-or-death decision, and I needed to get a grip. When I finally called Loren, just hearing his voice made me cry.

"She's going to be fine," he said, as he always did. "When I get there, she'll be fine."

"No, Loren, this is different," I said. "I don't think she's going to make it."

"Pat, she always pulls through," he said gently. I wanted to believe him, but in my heart I couldn't.

Between fifteen-minutes visits, I sat in the waiting room. That first night someone sent a chaplain to talk with me. I had been presented with the option of signing a do-not-resuscitate order, or DNR, which meant that if Hydeia went into crisis again or crashed, they had my permission to simply let her go. Intellectually, I understood why, but I wasn't ready because I didn't believe that Hydeia was ready. As I explained to the chaplain, Hydeia had been playing happily less than twenty-four hours ago. I did not want to ever give up on her, not only because I loved her but also because I had heard so many parents whose children had died on DNRs later question their decisions. I'd heard too many say things like, "If I wasn't so upset then," or "If I'd only been thinking more clearly then about it."

"It's okay to know when it's enough," he said kindly. "You shouldn't feel guilty."

"It's not that," I replied. "I'm just not sure that this is the time to take this step. I don't feel, at this point, that her quality of life warrants this." The truth was, at that point, we had no idea what her quality of life might be. "I just don't want to give up."

"You shouldn't worry what other people might think about your decision," he said, guessing, I suppose, at my reason for holding on.

"I really never cared about what other people think," I answered. "I'm just not ready to do this."

He left, and I guess he went upstairs and told someone that I was a little hard to reach. Before too long, another chaplain appeared in the waiting room, but after a cool reception, he gave up quickly. Next up: a third chaplain, this one a black woman. Aha! I thought. Now I know what this is about. I was getting annoyed at this point, but she was very kind. "You know, this is a hard situation, but you've got to know that it's okay to know when she's had enough. You don't want to be selfish."

That hit me, because I had often thought about this day and wondered if I would give up because it was the right thing to do or if I would react to being so tired, so overwhelmed, and so afraid. The truth was, however, I was not convinced that this was the day. Finally, though, I'd had enough. "As far as I'm concerned, I haven't heard the fat lady sing yet," I said. "I want whatever can be done to be done. And if we bring her back, she can't do anything, and she has another crisis, then I might be at the point of saying enough is enough. But don't come to me no more. And don't send anyone else down here."

"Mrs. Broadbent, we're not trying to coerce you. We just don't want you not to know what to do—"

"Fine. I'm doing what I want to do. Now, please, leave me alone."

I stayed awake all night; Hydeia did not wake up. The next morning, Lori rushed up to me in the waiting room. Checking her computer when she came in, she had seen that Hydeia was in ICU. "Why didn't you call me?" she asked. "You know I would have come in and talked with you, sat with you."

"What the fuck could you have done?" I asked angrily, and immediately regretted it. Lori was a very special person, and I know she would have done anything for Hydeia and our family. I was just so angry and so afraid of losing control, getting swept away, and making the wrong decision. My anger became my defense. I understood that people wanted to help me, but their warmth and caring seemed to sharpen the pain. Fortunately, Lori understood me.

On the second day, Hydeia opened her eyes. When I asked, "Can you hear me?" she said nothing, yet when I asked her to move her arms, her toes, her legs, she could. She kept staring at the Betty Boop cartoon on television. Maybe she could hear me but couldn't speak, I thought. "Say something to Mommy," I implored, but nothing. Half in panic, half in fear, I said, "Well, okay, then. If you don't want to talk to me, I'm leaving."

"No!" she screamed. Hydeia was back, and, miraculously, without having sustained any permanent damage. Before long, she was up and about, just Hydeia again in every way. I, however, had been changed. In those days, I learned to appreciate what it really means to say that life is too short. I started letting go of things that I believed should matter to me but didn't. I started doing some of the things I'd always wanted to do, like loosen up on the housework and wear my hair in braids. Whatever tolerance I had for bullshit got even smaller. Was I the mother from hell that some people might have thought I was? Well, if asking questions, making demands, and speaking your

mind are the requirements for that title, then I guess I was. However, I think that's all just semantics. I was a warrior.

By 1991 our hard work started paying off: Reach Out was
slowly but surely becoming a real place. Little did we know
then that the house the church leased to us would not be our
permanent home. Within that first year, we would be forced to
leave the church property we and our volunteers had so lovingly
renovated. Still, we were fulfilling the mission Diana, Cindy, and
I had first envisioned. Not one for false modesty, I knew we had
accomplished something big. Before we opened our doors, we
knew that we would change people's lives. Still, we were stunned
to learn we had been chosen to receive the Pediatric AIDS Foundation's A Time for Heroes Award months before Reach Out
opened. Given the tremendous role Elizabeth Glaser and the Pediatric AIDS Foundation had already played in our children's
lives, the award held special meaning for us. The event also
marked the beginning of a very special relationship with the
foundation that continues today.

Paula Zahn presented Diana, Cindy, and me with our awards,
live on *CBS This Morning*. Afterward the three of us sat with
our kids and talked to Paula about Reach Out and pediatric
AIDS. I was never exactly nervous speaking in public, but during this show I misspoke and said that Reach Out stood for "Receiving Every AIDS Child's Hurt is Our Ultimate Task" instead
of "Relieving." When the taping was over, Diana kidded me
about it, saying she thought we'd all received enough already.
The award itself, which I'm looking at as I write this, is a heavy
black iron abstract sculpture, about eighteen inches tall and
twenty pounds. Inscribed on it are the words "Pediatric AIDS
Foundation Hero Award given to Patricia Broadbent 1991 for
Outstanding Leadership, Compassion, and Courage in the Battle Against Pediatric AIDS." A few years later, Hydeia also
would be given the award for her work as an AIDS activist.

The funny thing is that both Hydeia and I consider Elizabeth our hero. Although I had seen her at that first pediatric AIDS conference and she had given Hydeia a PAF tape of celebrities singing lullabies, we didn't really get to know each other until the summer of 1991, after the award. Elizabeth worked closely with Dr. Pizzo and was often at NIH, but our paths didn't cross there, because she found it difficult to visit the Children's Inn. In fact, the only time she ever went there, it was to visit Hydeia.

Hydeia and I were invited to attend the annual celebrity-studded Time for Heroes picnic in Los Angeles that summer. Hydeia was not feeling particularly strong because her red-blood-cell count was dropping, leaving her weak and tired. She wanted so badly to attend that Dr. Pizzo said okay, but only under the condition that we get her monitored at UCLA several times.

The picnic was a carnival held at the estate of billionaire philanthropist Ken Roberts, with games, food, clowns, music—everything a child could want. We have attended the picnic every year since, and we always look forward to it. Dozens of celebrities—actors, sports stars, music people—attend, and through the years, we've met Robin Williams, Rhea Perlman, Barbra Streisand, Tom Hanks, Geena Davis, Courteney Cox, Whoopi Goldberg, Sugar Ray Leonard, Steven Spielberg, Dustin Hoffman, Brooke Shields, Candice Bergen, Drew Barrymore, and others. One year Debbie Allen held a dance class for the children. The celebrities played with the kids, posed for pictures, and helped make the day special. It was here that Hydeia and Elizabeth forged their unique and special bond.

Before that first picnic, Hydeia participated in a press conference with Elizabeth. Although Hydeia was very ill, she followed Elizabeth everywhere. Elizabeth, who always pronounced Hydeia "hie-DAY-uh," was warm but reserved. I know how much Hydeia reminded Elizabeth of her daughter, Ariel. Elizabeth's book, *In the Absence of Angels*, was published in 1991, not long after this picnic. In it, she talked openly of her ongoing, overwhelming grief over Ariel's death at age seven in August 1988. By then, Elizabeth's own health was starting to show the effects of the virus, and she was very concerned about her son, Jake, who was a few months younger than Hydeia and had not yet developed AIDS. Despite her own sorrow and worry, Elizabeth kept fighting, for Jake and for every child. More than once I wondered how many people in Elizabeth's situation would have devoted the time she had left to traveling to Washington, lobbying, and giving so much of herself to the cause. In 1991, living for ten years with the virus was rare. With only AZT (which she had to stop taking) and ddI in the medical arsenal, it was only a matter of time before the virus won.

As much as Elizabeth liked Hydeia, I could see that being around her was sometimes painful, too. I tried to explain this to Hydeia as sensitively as I could. "Sometimes Elizabeth just needs a little time to herself," I told Hydeia.

"She'll be okay," Hydeia would say. "It's okay."

After we had spent more time with Elizabeth, a year or so later, she wrote Hydeia a beautiful letter. In it, she said that she and Hydeia were like soldiers fighting the same war. She told Hydeia that she admired her and mentioned how much she reminded her of Ariel. Somewhere written between the lines, I got the impression that Elizabeth was trying to say, If I'm not always that warm toward you, it's because it hurts. I read the letter to Hydeia, and she simply said, "I know. It's okay."

I remember 1991 as the year that so many children died. In terms of her health, Hydeia was still running in place. More than once, medical crises and unplanned hospital stays squashed plans to celebrate her seventh birthday that June. Her LIP made it difficult for her to breathe sometimes, and she couldn't fly without oxygen tanks. I had noticed that sometimes when she slept her nostrils would flare out just like a little frightened rabbit's. When I told the doctor about that and the fact that she often woke up suddenly right after drifting off to sleep, they hooked her up to a device that measured her blood oxygen level. Sure enough, as she drifted off to sleep, you could see the oxygen level drop steadily until it was so low that she was literally suffocating and would startle awake, gasping for breath. It turns out that she had lost about 60 or 70 percent of her normal lung function.

Around this time, Hydeia also went on an intensive course of corticosteroid treatment. Before we went to NIH, Dr. K. had put her on brief corticosteroid regimens whenever her LIP flared up. Corticosteroids were the only effective treatment for LIP, but they are notoriously hard on the body, so you want to use them for as short a period as you can. Not only do they suppress immune function but they also tend to cause massive, rapid bloating and the characteristic "moon face." Seemingly overnight, my skinny little wisp of a thing disappeared and a chubby, round-faced girl emerged. The change could be so rapid that a dress that was hanging off her in the morning would be bursting at the seams by the end of the day. If you saw the *I Need a Friend* tape Lori made with her at NIH and then saw her sitting beside me, plump in her dark red corduroy dress on *CBS This Morning,* you would never guess it was the same child. Fortunately for Hydeia, the corticosteroids improved her breathing immensely and she did not suffer the debilitating depression or wild mood swings some people experience on them. The other positive side effect was the increase in her appetite. Not that she ever got to the point where she was eating normally, but she was eating more. Hydeia would be on a constant course of corticosteroids for the next three years.

Amazingly, she never once complained. In fact, she complains more today about a minor headache than she ever did about a major surgical procedure when she was younger. She could be starving, burning up with fever, or experiencing severe pain, but she never made a peep. I realized that she had probably never felt truly well since the day she was born. What would be difficult, uncomfortable, even unbearable for most of us was, to Hydeia, just normal. I think this explains her surprising lack of memory about these years.

Despite the havoc AIDS wreaked in our lives, there were bright moments, too. One of Hydeia's friends was a little boy named Dougie. I became quite close to his mother, June, who was also infected but refused to be tested. What was most amazing about these kids is that no matter how sick and debilitated they may have been, their personalities shone through. Dougie was a real character. He was like a little old man. Like Hydeia, life had made him old and granted him wisdom far beyond his years. Also like Hydeia, he had a habit of addressing adults as if he, too, were an adult and had no qualms about letting you know what he wanted.

Hydeia and Dougie were sharing a room after one of her lung biopsies. We'd had a particularly bad night, with Hydeia waking up due to lack of oxygen, chest pain, and dizziness. She was put on a pulse oxygen monitor, which would sound an alarm whenever her blood oxygen dropped below a certain level. Between that and a chorus of machines that constantly beeped, whirred, hummed, and occasionally sounded alarms, none of us got any rest.

From the next bed, Dougie—a shrewd little observer— watched it all. Although just seven or eight, he didn't fail to notice how peacefully Hydeia rested after she got a shot of morphine. The next morning a British doctor, Dr. Tudor Williams, stopped by to check on her and on Dougie. He talked first to Hydeia, then asked Dougie how he was doing.

"I'm hurting," Dougie said. "You have to give me something more than Tylenol." I swear, the kids up there knew more about the meds than most of us parents.

"Okay, we'll give you something a little stronger today," Dr. Williams said, then turned to walk out of the room.

Suddenly Dougie called out, "Dr. Tudor Williams?"

"Yes, Dougie?"

In a perfectly grown-up way, he said, "I want some of that shit Hydeia had last night."

June and I looked at each other in disbelief, then broke out laughing. This was what June referred to as "a Dougie thing."

Sometime around Easter 1992 Dougie died. Although Hydeia was touched by the death of any child she knew, Dougie was among a handful of very special friends. The poor little guy went through hell before he passed, battling massive infections and progressive liver failure. We were on our way to NIH when June called me from there to tell me that Dougie was going downhill rapidly. She was distraught, struggling to find that invisible point in time when death ceases to be a force to resist and becomes the unwelcome inevitable. June's mother was standing right beside her and got on the phone. "Pat, if you could, tell June that she needs to tell Dougie to let go and tell him that she's going to be okay."

Now, years ago, if anyone had ever told me that children have a hard time letting go until they know in their hearts that their parents will be all right, I wouldn't have believed it. Yet I have witnessed this phenomenon more times than you could count. I believe that it explains how a child who, medically speaking, should not be able to survive will keep on fighting. In the hopes of shortening Dougie's suffering, the doctors had discontinued all of his meds; he was on oxygen only. I understood that June's mother was asking this favor of me because she loved her daughter and her grandson. Still, it was hard for me to persuade another parent to see a reality that I wasn't so sure I would be able to accept.

When I talked with June, she said, "Pat, I just can't bring myself to tell him that it's okay or that I'll be okay."

I understood, but I said, "June, listen. You need to seize this moment. I'm not saying to rush it, and you can decide not to listen to the doctors or even to your mom. But at some point you are going to have to let him know."

When we arrived at NIH the next day, Dougie was gone. June

told me how she had cradled him in her arms, told him that she would be all right, that he shouldn't worry, and that she loved him. He looked at her, turned his head, fell asleep, and passed away.

Of course, NIH wanted to keep Dougie there for autopsy, but for some reason they wanted June to leave the Children's Inn. She just couldn't. "Don't leave him," I told her. "You come and stay with me in my room, but don't do anything you don't feel comfortable doing." She stayed for another day or so. Before she left, we hugged and I told her to call me whenever she wanted. The next time we spoke, right before Dougie's funeral, June told me about how, due to some delay or mix-up, they weren't sure exactly when he would be home. Because of the Easter holidays, it wasn't clear when the funeral could take place. After everything, you'd expect June to be upset. Instead, the two of us shared a laugh when June quipped, "Well, it's just another Dougie thing. Like always, Dougie is in control." Not everyone would appreciate the humor there, but I did. June understood that to truly grieve a child, you had to embrace everything about him, especially what made you smile.

Hydeia took Dougie's death very hard. As she grew older, I think she came to understand death a little better with each passing, and in some ways that made it harder than it had been when she was younger. She wrote June a letter about Dougie and added that she looked forward to seeing him again when she was nine. Reading that, my heart skipped a beat. What was she thinking? What did she know?

A couple of years later, when Hydeia was about nine, I decided to plan her funeral. It might sound odd, but I felt that the last thing I wanted to think about if she passed was her funeral. I didn't want to find myself negotiating terms with funeral salesmen or making decisions about anything. By then, Hydeia had become well enough known that I knew media would be involved. Lori at NIH promised to handle that aspect.

I admit it was a little strange to be sitting in my living room with a funeral director talking about flowers and coffins. I know he thought it a little odd. Loren, who thought it was morbid, wouldn't participate but didn't object to my doing it. I reminded him that he hadn't talked to a mother who had been manipulated and pressured into doing everything from spending more than she could afford to not dressing her child in the outfit she chose. The one word you often heard from parents who had lost a child was *regret* over the loss of control. I knew exactly what I would want and what I would not. I think the funeral director probably found me a little bit too cool, but he had no idea what I'd gone through to get to this point. Not being able to bear the thought of leaving a child in the ground, I decided that Hydeia would be cremated. I would disperse some of her ashes in special places and hold on to some to keep.

I'd once asked Hydeia, "If you could disappear into anything you wanted to disappear in, what would you like to go as?"

"A little angel," she replied, I'm sure not knowing what I was asking or why.

She had begun collecting angel figurines, and when I noticed that some of them were hollow with holes in the bottom, I knew where Hydeia would always be, long after she was gone.

FIVE

he funny—and astonishing and inspiring—thing about Hydeia was that for all the death around her, for all the times it had grazed her, she had no intention of dying anytime soon. As she would later say in a speech, "I have a leash on AIDS. AIDS does not have a leash on me." Somewhere inside her there flowed hope and determination. Still, there were those times when I had to wonder if she knew something that I didn't. Late in the summer of 1991, when her health finally got back on track, she announced, "I want to get married."

This didn't surprise me, because practically from the time she could walk, Hydeia was Little Miss Domestic. She would prepare play meals out of plastic fruits and vegetables. She was the Julia Child of the Fisher-Price kitchen set. The Christmas she found a little battery-powered Corvette she could drive around the neighborhood under the tree, she pouted because Santa had forgotten the play ironing board. The Christmas before, Hydeia had asked for a wedding gown, and we had given her a play dress-up version: a little halter top, a half-slip-style skirt, a veil, and some other accessories. From the moment she got it, she started talking about getting married. Thinking this was just Hydeia being a little girl, I replied, "Oh, you will when you get older."

"No, Mommy, I want to get married now."

"Okay, fine. For your birthday, we'll do a wedding." I was thinking more along the lines of what they call a Tom Thumb wedding, a pretend wedding instead of a mermaid party or whatever the popular party theme was back in 1991. "So who do you want to marry?"

"Tyler," she said, and that was fine with me, because their birthdays are only a day apart and we had planned to celebrate them together anyway. Although it was now August, Hydeia had been through so much that summer, I was happy to give her the party she wanted.

Before I knew it, though, this wedding birthday party started taking on a life of its own. Hydeia invited my best friend, Rita, who promised to fly in from San Diego. Cindy, whose brother-in-law loves to bake, planned to make a fabulous wedding cake, and our little bride wanted a gown, a veil, and a ring—the works. A friend of mine modified Hydeia's wedding costume with the addition of a balloon-style skirt and yards of billowing nylon mesh. My oldest son, Kendall, wrote the vows, in which Hydeia and Tyler would promise to be friends for life, and agreed to officiate. We really went into what I call "family mode," and everyone took it as seriously as Hydeia did. Rita bought her real flowers for her bouquet and let me know that she thought my slacks did not constitute proper attire for the mother of the bride. So we all got dressed up, too.

With all the uncertainty in our lives, the one thing I had learned was to seize the moment. We didn't have a lot of time to make fancy plans, because no one could promise that we wouldn't be on a plane bound for Washington the next day. In the midst of it all, someone close to me asked why I was doing all this, and I answered, "Because this is what Hydeia wants,

DEAR DOUGIE,

I just learned that you passed away. I feel very sad. I feel that all my friends die. But I have more friends. I will write and write to your mom. I will write to you too.

I want you to know about all the things that I will always remember about you. You always listened to rap music. You were always nice to me, but you weren't always nice to everyone else. I loved you because you were sweet and fun.

I think that one day I will die too. I don't know when that day will be. When I die I might be 9 years old and you will be 9 years old too. So we will be the same age and I will show you my friends in Heaven and I will share my friends in Heaven with you.

I love you. I will always love you.

> Hydeia
> Age eight

and who knows if she'll ever get to have her own wedding. Maybe she knows something I don't know."

The "wedding day" came, and we all gathered at Cindy's house. The guests included not only family and friends but also many of the doctors, nurses, and other home health care nurses who worked with Hydeia and Tyler. With Keisha as her maid of honor, Hydeia walked down the aisle to where Tyler and his best man, his brother Rocky, waited. Hydeia was in her glory, with her hair up in braids and her long white gown trailing a few inches behind her. As short as she was, she stood a couple of inches taller than Tyler, who looked every bit the little gentleman in dark pants, a white shirt, vest, and bow tie. Cindy's brother-in-law had gone to town on the wedding cake—perched atop it were a black girl bride and a white, blond boy groom.

The ceremony may have been a pretend wedding, but it was a real expression of Hydeia and Tyler's friendship. They share a special bond, and it has been interesting to watch them growing up together. After they made their promises to help each other, Kendall said, "I now pronounce you friends for life. You may hug the bride." Everyone applauded as they hugged, and then it was time for cake. Hydeia cut the cake carefully, and once she and Tyler had been served, they fed each other yellow cake, and neatly, too. Of course, we videotaped the event, and the tape ends with the "honeymooners" taking off down the sidewalk on bikes strewn with crepe paper and strings of tin cans. If you look carefully, you can see Tyler's training wheels.

A year or so later, when *20/20* came to the house to start interviewing and researching for a segment on pediatric AIDS, the producer asked to see home videos. After the program aired, with a few moments of Hydeia's wedding footage, we were contacted by other television shows, including *The Jerry Springer Show,* which invited Hydeia and Tyler on to reenact the event about a year after that. Now, this was back when Jerry's show still had more in common with Oprah and Sally Jessy Raphaël than with World Federation Wrestling. For this, however, the show's producers went all out and had a real miniature wedding gown and veil designed and created for Hydeia. It was made of the finest material, with clouds of lace sprinkled with hand-sewn beads, pearls, and sequins. If the event cost anything less than five thousand dollars, I would be surprised. As lovely as it all was, however, I couldn't help but think what we at Reach Out could have done with at least a portion of that money. This was one of my first lessons in the hoopla of media. The Springer show paid to fly all of us—Loren, me, Hydeia, Keisha, Kendall and his wife, Mary, Cindy and her husband, Larry, Tyler, and their other four children (Tanya, Rocky, Tim, and Jamie) to Chicago for the taping. The stage overflowed with flowers and all the wedding trappings. This time Hydeia and Tyler vowed to be "eternal friends." At one point during the interview portion, Loren and I were seated to Hydeia's right. On her left was Tyler, and on the other side of him sat Cindy and Larry. When Jerry found out about the year's difference in the kids' ages, he remarked that Hydeia seemed to prefer "younger men."

"Yeah," she answered nonchalantly. "They're pretty easy to boss around." A few minutes later she added, "All the women in my family boss the men around." This was met by a round of knowing laughter and a resigned expression from her father.

By then, Hydeia had done enough public speaking that on any stage, in front of any audience, she was the epitome of cool. Her penchant for playing dress-up translated into a desire to always look her best in public. She amassed a closetful of outfits for every occasion, complete with accessories, including the color-coordinated backpack or shoulder bag that held her medication pump. Through the Pediatric AIDS Foundation and NIH, Hydeia's face became familiar, seen on training films, pubic service announcements, and videos produced for AIDS organizations. Whenever any news organization wanted a story on pediatric AIDS, they went to Elizabeth Glaser's foundation, and Hydeia's name invariably came up. I've always felt that when it came to raising awareness about AIDS, Hydeia should do only what she wanted to do. For her, it wasn't just about being a "poster child" for the cause. It really was about saving lives, if not the lives of the people in her audience, then the lives of their future children. Even at the age of eight, Hydeia had a vision and a mission. Unlike too many children I have seen through the years, she refused to see herself—or permit others to see her—as a victim.

Sometime in early 1992 we learned that television journalist Linda Ellerbee was interested in speaking with Hydeia about participating in a special on AIDS she was producing for the kids' channel Nickelodeon. In November 1991 basketball legend Earvin "Magic" Johnson had revealed that he had contracted HIV. This was a landmark event in the history of AIDS awareness, the first time an athlete had come forward and admitted that he had contracted the virus through unprotected heterosexual sex. The revelation unleashed an unprecedented outpouring of sympathy and understanding, and many observers believe that it marked a subtle shift in the way the American public came to view the disease. Until then, the public perception of a person with AIDS was a distant glimpse of a dying Rock Hudson being wheeled into an ambulance or an obviously gaunt Liberace. This was the first time a famous person with the virus had come forward before the disease ravaged him, while he was still healthy and active. Johnson showed people that a diagnosis was not an immediate death sentence, and that having HIV/AIDS did not preclude hope or happiness.

Yes, the nation as a whole started seeing HIV/AIDS in a less stigmatizing light after Johnson came forward. Certainly, it took courage on his part to do what he did, months and perhaps even years before he really had to. Because of Magic Johnson, people who had never thought much about HIV/AIDS were doing so. Because of Magic Johnson, the danger of infection through heterosexual contact became real. However, as the world applauded and embraced Magic Johnson, some of us who had been living with the disease saw it all a bit differently. Why, I wondered, did people with HIV/AIDS only become "acceptable" and worthy of compassion once the disease became associated with a professional athlete? A professional athlete, by the way, who made it very clear that he had contracted the virus by being sexually promiscuous and not taking the precautions that Surgeon General C. Everett Koop had urged as early as 1986. Why, we wondered, were the same people who would just as soon run a child with AIDS out of school or a gay adult with AIDS out of town suddenly deciding that they could now accept someone with AIDS? That suddenly because Magic had it, they could be cool? Why? Because he was rich? Because he led the Lakers? Because he got it in a "normal" way? It made no sense to me.

As the mother of a child with AIDS, I found it depressing to realize that the suffering and the deaths of hundreds of thousands of men, women, and children somehow just weren't "enough" to inspire the nation's compassion or action. It was distressing to think that the years of educational effort put forth by people like Elizabeth Glaser, Surgeon General Koop, writer-activist Larry Kramer, and dozens of others could not make a shadow of the impression Magic Johnson did. Let me be clear, though: My problem was not with Magic Johnson personally but with the idea that we live in a society where the meaning of the message depends so much on the messenger. These were my feelings about Magic Johnson before Linda Ellerbee called.

Linda had contacted Elizabeth Glaser about gathering a group of kids, preferably around the age of eleven or older. The show would present information on HIV/AIDS in an informal group discussion format, with the children asking Magic questions and Linda moderating. Linda was keen to find a few children who had HIV/AIDS and would be comfortable talking about it on television. Unfortunately, at that time, there weren't

many such children around. Elizabeth immediately thought of
Hydeia, but she was only eight. Apparently, Elizabeth spoke so
highly of Hydeia that Linda agreed to give her a call and talk
with her anyway. I spoke briefly to Linda, then handed the telephone to Hydeia. Linda asked her what question she would ask
Magic. By then, Hydeia had done enough public speaking to
have some understanding of how difficult it was to convince
people—and especially children—that HIV was their problem,
too. Even at that young age, Hydeia knew that—for better or
worse—people judged the message by the messenger. I won't say
that Hydeia knew everything there was to know about the facts
of life, but she couldn't talk about HIV without talking about
sex. So she understood enough about how Magic had contracted the virus to have one very simple question. As she put it
to Linda, "I want to ask, What makes Magic Johnson think people will listen when he didn't listen? I want to tell him that if he
wants me to, I'll go with him, because people listen to me."

From a child's point of view, this struck me as a totally credi-
ble and valid question. I don't know what Linda thought of that,
because we never discussed it. As far as we knew, that would be
Hydeia's question when her turn to ask Magic came around.

The show was taped in New Jersey, so Hydeia, Pepe, and I
flew into Newark the day before. The casual studio set looked
like a cross between a classroom and a big family room. Johnson
sat to the left of about ten or twelve children ranging from ten
through their teens. Hydeia was by far the youngest, and between being so small for her age and having that chubby-baby
steroid look, she appeared much younger. Hydeia was one of
two children on the show who had AIDS. Another child was the
brother of a boy we knew who had AIDS but had been too ill to
participate.

As the taping began, none of the children knew who had the
virus and who didn't. The children's questions were intelligent,
and Magic and Linda gave their answers in a calm, reassuring

way. It was a wonderful program, and "A Conversation with Magic" won the prestigious Cable Ace Award for best news special of 1992. (At the time, I didn't know that just ten days before the taping Linda had undergone a double mastectomy for breast cancer.)

For Hydeia, however, the memory of the program is bittersweet. The plan had been for all the children on the show to raise their hand, with Magic calling on them in an order they had determined. During a break in the taping, when Hydeia hadn't yet been called on, I asked Linda, "Are you going to let her talk?" Linda assured me that Hydeia would get her chance. As the taping continued, however, Magic didn't call on her, although she sat not more than ten feet from him and raised her hand persistently.

I could see Hydeia getting impatient as she thrust her chubby arm into the air again and again. Magic called on the kids to one side of her and the other, and behind her, but never on Hydeia. Since Hydeia had started talking publicly about AIDS, she always made sure she had her facts straight. So you can imagine the look on her face (and on mine) when one of the children asked Magic, "What does *AIDS* stand for?" and he replied that that was "a little technical" for him, and Linda answered instead. Finally, toward the end of the taping, Hydeia could not contain herself and she burst into tears. Everyone, including Magic, tried to comfort her, and between sobs, she made a statement about kids with HIV or AIDS being just like other kids. Everyone thought she was crying about that and the fact that she had AIDS. In fact, though, she was furious that she had not been able to ask her question.

I called Elizabeth immediately and demanded that Johnson call me. She gently tried to dissuade me from confronting him. "Magic is new at this," she said. "We're all on the same team, Pat."

"I don't feel that way, Elizabeth," I replied. "He owes Hydeia an apology for ignoring her question and making her so upset that she feels she's been publicly humiliated."

A little back-and-forth followed, but before the day was over my telephone rang and a voice said, "This is Magic. I was wondering if I could talk to Hydeia."

"I don't think Hydeia wants to talk to Magic," I replied. "I think she wants to talk to Earvin."

Hydeia got on the phone and asked him straight up why he had not called on her to ask her question. He said nothing but offered to "do some things together" with her in the future. I wasn't surprised when over the next ten years nothing came of that, and neither was Hydeia. (Coincidentally, as I write this chapter, Hydeia is preparing to tape a segment for a show celebrating the tenth anniversary of Nickelodeon's *Nick News*.)

When Hydeia saw the program on television several weeks later, she was devastated. She had worked half of her life to change the way the world looked at people with AIDS. For her, it was not about asking for pity and making people feel sorry for her. It was about empowerment, acceptance, and living with dignity. Yet here she was seeing herself on the television screen reduced to sobbing and the whole world thinking it was because she had AIDS. She was not only embarrassed but also worried that people would think she was a hypocrite. Here she was telling everyone that AIDS was nothing to be ashamed of, that she felt happy, powerful, and undiminished by the disease, and then she's blubbering all over the place before millions of viewers.

Hydeia's activism also had a personal side, and in early 1992 it led all of us onto an unexpected path. Hydeia was suffering from infections and complications, one right after the other. In addition to the regular visits to NIH (which were now down to about once every three weeks), she had countless stays at the

University Medical Center here at home. Like most girls her age, Hydeia was drawn to babies, and whenever she felt up to it, she would go visit babies in the ward. There one January day, she discovered and fell in love with a baby girl named Patricia, who was born with AIDS. The hospital knew who Patricia's mother was, but rarely did anyone from the baby's family come to visit her. I think Hydeia found it easy to imagine herself in Patricia's place. I knew that once Patricia had achieved a reasonable degree of health, she was destined to join other babies like her in foster care or temporary state placements like Child Haven (which by then had a growing caseload of HIV-positive babies).

At that time, and for several years to come, I was still taking in on a temporary basis babies who were HIV-positive or who had AIDS. Dealing with it had become second nature to me, and as much as we all enjoyed having a new baby around, the idea of our adopting another child—HIV or no HIV—was out of the question. When it came to Patricia, however, Hydeia had other ideas. In her heart she had already "adopted" this baby. She spent every minute she could in Patricia's room, playing with her and talking to her. When Hydeia was not in the hospital, she was calling the nurses on the telephone to find out how Patricia was doing. Then I noticed a funny thing: Hydeia would go into the hospital one day with a fever, then the next day she would be fine. It was almost as if being around Patricia had a healing effect on her.

One day Hydeia dropped the bomb: "Can we adopt Patricia?"

You can imagine the look on my face, but before I could answer, Hydeia said, "If we don't bring her home, she'll die."

As we would find out later, Hydeia was more right than she knew. Still, it seemed out of the question for us, at least for now. "Hydeia, I understand how you feel, but we have to think about this," I said. "What would happen if the baby got sick here at home while I was with you up at NIH? I couldn't be in two places at the same time. How could we take care of both of you?"

Undaunted, Hydeia replied, "I promise, Mom, if you bring her home, I won't ever get sick again."

What could I say? Like Hydeia, Patricia was very small for her age, and weak. She hardly made a sound, and she didn't seem to be hearing well, either. In fact, there was some suspicion that she might be deaf. She had weighed seven pounds at birth but had quickly become a classic case of failure to thrive. At four months, when she should have gained at least five pounds, she had gained just two. She had problems with reflux, meaning essentially that she regurgitated whatever she ate. Consequently, Patricia had to sleep in an almost sitting position and was always at risk for pneumonia and even death from inhaling her food. She had an apnea monitor, because she would stop breathing when she slept. This wasn't going to be easy.

I knew from speaking to the baby's social worker that the mother was not yet entirely out of the picture. We agreed that we would take baby Patricia temporarily, just until her mother could take her or they found her another home. You might think it an odd coincidence that this baby's name was also Patricia, but there's more. After we brought Patricia home with us, on April 1, 1992, I started trying to find out more about her mother. One day the social worker assigned to Patricia's case mentioned that Patricia's mother had named her after a woman she had a lot of respect for, a woman who ran the Boys Club and once helped her get on her feet: That woman was me. It turned out that I knew Patricia's mother, first as a young girl and later as an expectant mother at Reach Out. In fact, that previous November, we had helped her put together a nice Thanksgiving dinner for her family and got her and her three older children a tree and gifts for Christmas. Now that baby she was carrying then was living in my home.

Knowing this, I held out hope that Patricia could one day be reunited with her mother. As I learned more about this woman, though, the chances of that occurring dwindled rapidly. Illiterate, overwhelmed, and afraid, she was convinced that the medication she had been given during her pregnancy to help protect her unborn baby would kill her, so she didn't take it. After we brought Patricia home, I reached out to her mother and arranged for them to spend time together. At first she came every other day, and I showed her how to bathe the baby. I explained the numerous medications Patricia was on and why they were important. I even color-coded the bottles, so that she could know what to give her baby when.

As you can imagine, Patricia's mother brought many different emotions to these visits, but the one that overtook all others was fear. She was afraid of the disease, distrustful of the doctors and the meds, and easily overwhelmed. What started as a promising possibility gradually faded into a lost cause, as Patricia's mother visited less and less often. Since we hadn't yet adopted Patricia legally, I couldn't refuse her mother's request to take her for special occasions. Soon, though, it was apparent that the only time she was interested in being Patricia's mother was when she wanted to show the baby off. Months passed between visits. Every time Patricia left with her, she would scream and cry, because she didn't know this woman. Finally, I told her, "If you're going to be involved, be involved. If not, then move on." She moved on.

Because Patricia began going to NIH at such an early age, her experience of living with HIV is entirely different from Hydeia's. When Patricia was about six months, we had a Portocath put in for her meds and drawing blood, and she began taking AZT. Fortunately, she tolerated it very well and has never been seriously ill.

Hydeia adored being a big sister to Patricia, whom she treated like her very own baby. Patricia was small enough to fit into Hydeia's doll stroller and playpen. With her big, luminous eyes and beautiful face, Patricia was truly a living doll. Whenever Patricia needed to have a shot, a blood draw, an MRI, or any other procedure, Hydeia was right there, talking her through it. Even today, Hydeia is more vigilant about making sure that Patricia takes her meds than she is about herself.

Once Patricia got old enough to talk, it was obvious that she and Hydeia couldn't have been more different. I had grown accustomed to Hydeia, who rarely complained and always demonstrated a strong will to fight when she hit a medical crisis. In contrast, Patricia was not a complainer, but whenever she was sick, everyone knew about it. Whereas Hydeia could have a chest tube pulled out one minute and be up jumping off the hospital bed to go play the next, Patricia would not and could not be moved for any reason whatsoever once she decided she wasn't moving. Once when she had to be given general anesthesia to fill the cavities that developed after months of taking a very sugary medicine, I jokingly told the doctors, "You'd better be sure you do the breathing for her, because she won't do it herself." Hydeia I could pack up to fly cross-country on a day's notice, while it takes Patricia three hours just to get ready for school, because first she needs to work on her computer, read, do some writing, play a little, and so on.

In her own way, though, Patricia is a fighter. She is smart, independent, and feisty. I like to say she is a chip off her own unique little block. She blended into the family so completely, to look at her and her older siblings today, you would never guess they weren't blood. I remember her sitting with her much older siblings as they took turns telling "mama" jokes, trying to top each other, and joining in. She would see Hydeia on television and say, "Hydeia's in the TV! Get her out, Mommy!" (When Patricia misbehaved, I'd threaten to put her in the TV, too.) As early as age three, she let Hydeia know that she did not want or need to be hovered over. Even today, when Hydeia goes to one summer camp and Patricia to another, Hydeia will miss Patricia when she's gone. But when Patricia comes off the plane, the first thing she'll say is that she misses camp.

Despite their differences, the two are very close. While Patricia is open about the fact that she has AIDS, she has no interest in doing what Hydeia does. I have had people ask me if we adopted Patricia so that she could "take up" when or if Hydeia stops being an activist. The first time I heard that, I couldn't believe my ears. How could anyone be so insensitive? Not to mention stupid.

Though Hydeia would eventually make good on her promise not to get sick, there was still one major crisis ahead. Sometime in the summer of 1992 Hydeia suddenly began to behave in ways that were out of character. She was never what you would call a pushover; she always stood up for herself. Seemingly overnight, her assertiveness took on a nastier, sharper edge. Once she threw a board game at Keisha and hit her in the eye. More than once when I threatened to spank her, she replied defiantly, "Go ahead! You can spank me if you want to!" She could be screaming, cursing, and carrying on one minute, and then quiet, contrite, and totally unaware of what she had said or done just a few minutes later. It got so bad that Keisha—who was about twice as tall and twice as heavy as Hydeia—wouldn't even play with her, and we were careful not to let her be around Patricia without supervision.

When I mentioned this to the doctors up at NIH, they felt it was probably an emotional problem. After all, she was getting older and becoming increasingly more aware of what it meant to have AIDS and how she was different from other kids. That I could understand—to a point. However, as I told the doctors at NIH, even if that was true, my kids know better than to talk to me like that. Period. Though I didn't mean it literally, of course, I said, "One of my kids would have to be crazy to think I'd let them get away with this kind of behavior." Little did I know. Reassured that the behavior would probably pass, we went home, but not only did Hydeia's behavior get worse, it became downright scary.

One day she told me that she was talking to a person named

George. Several times we saw or overheard her carrying on a conversation with this imaginary friend. One day when she mentioned that she had talked to George, I asked her, "Well, what did George say?"

"I can't tell you what George said," she replied.

"Yes, you can tell Mommy."

"No, you'll get mad if I tell you."

"No," I said calmly, "I will not get mad if you tell me what George said."

Hydeia looked me squarely in the eye and said, "George said you were a bitch!"

George was quite a character. We were up at NIH, getting ready for an appointment at the clinic. Hydeia sat on the bed putting her socks on, then pulling them off, putting them on, pulling them off. "What is the matter?" I asked.

"I'm putting on my socks," she replied casually.

"Well, leave them on," I said. "We've got to go soon."

No sooner were the words out of my mouth than she was taking her socks off again, putting them on. I put them on her feet, told her to go into the bathroom, wash her face, and brush her teeth. As I got Patricia ready to go, I could hear Hydeia talking. I quietly approached the bathroom doorway and peeked in. There she was, standing before the mirror and talking as if she were addressing someone I couldn't see off to the side. But there was no one there. At least no one I could see.

When I finally got everyone dressed and ready, we started out to NIH. Hydeia was holding on to Patricia's stroller, and as she walked, she would fall.

"What's wrong with you?" I asked.

"George is tripping me," she said sincerely.

"Hydeia, please," I said. "Just let me get you up to the thirteenth floor. Just please stop this."

A minute later, she fell again. And again, and again. I stopped being annoyed and started getting scared. I picked her up, strapped her into the stroller with Patricia, and ran upstairs.

When I told the doctors what had happened, they drew blood and examined her. At one point Hydeia shouted at a nurse, "You've got to get up! You've got to get up!"

Baffled, the nurse asked, "What's the matter, Hydeia?"

"You're sitting on George!" Hydeia replied in a tone that implied this should have been obvious to anyone. "He's going to get mad! You better get up!"

The nurse got up, and then we heard Hydeia saying to George, "Don't say that to me. Don't say that to me."

When Lori came in, she asked Hydeia what George was saying. Again Hydeia told her that she couldn't say or I would get mad. Lori pressed her, and the answer could have been taken from the script for *The Exorcist*: F—k you, this, that—you get the idea. This was not my little girl.

Once the blood-test results were in, the doctors eliminated most of the possible causes of Hydeia's sudden psychosis. Only one explanation remained: The HIV had crossed into her brain. What that might mean no one could say exactly, but I knew from seeing other kids that none of it would be good. There was only one medication with the power to defeat HIV in the brain, and Dr. Pizzo knew I did not want Hydeia to take it: AZT. Despite Patricia's success with AZT, my reservations about the drug for Hydeia were many and firm. It is a highly toxic drug that can break down normal muscle tissue, including the heart, if not closely monitored. It has a tendency to destroy platelets and white cells, and it can cause liver problems, which Hydeia already had. However, Dr. Pizzo explained, if these symptoms were caused by the HIV crossing into Hydeia's brain, things would only get worse. There might be more neurological symptoms; she might even lose the ability to walk. Knowing how I felt, Dr. Pizzo promised that if the side effects were intolerable, we would stop it. The bottom line was, however, that there was no other choice. Without the AZT, Hydeia's condition surely would deteriorate.

I agonized over the decision, but in the end I knew we had to try it, and I held my breath as we waited for the AZT to take effect. Ever watchful, I scrutinized and analyzed every possible sign. To my relief, Hydeia tolerated the AZT very well, and George, along with her other strange behaviors, disappeared practically overnight.

After that, Hydeia kept the promise she had made before we brought Patricia home: She stayed relatively healthy. The years of fighting near-constant infections, complications, and other AIDS-associated problems miraculously ended. Don't ask me how, but they did. Now, this is not to say that problems didn't crop up. Hydeia was still prone to infections, still taking multiple meds and undergoing procedures. The difference was that suddenly it felt as if there was some breathing room, enough time between crises that we could enjoy periods of living what resembled a normal family life.

When your child has intense medical needs, you learn to regard doctors in a different light. More than simply professionals who help—and sometimes even save—your child, they become your allies, soldiers fighting alongside you against this disease. Over the years, Dr. K. and I had developed a relationship of mutual respect and appreciation. I wasn't always the most patient mother he dealt with, but we had come to understand each other. When we learned that Dr. K. was leaving to work in another part of the country, Diana, Cindy, and I were devastated. Who would take his place? It wasn't just a matter of finding a doctor willing to take on pediatric AIDS cases, though that would be hard enough. When you looked at all the ways Dr. K. had helped make our situations more manageable—like always arranging for us to bypass the emergency room in a crisis—it was hard to imagine anyone else fully taking his place.

Somehow, word got around of a new doctor in town, Dr. Lisa

Bechtel. Dr. Lisa, as we soon began to call her, was intrigued by
the idea of treating children with AIDS. However, she hadn't
been trained in that area and had no experience. Diana, Cindy,
and I embarked on a carefully organized campaign to convince
her that she was needed. When I told Dr. Pizzo about her, he
opened a fellowship so that she could train at NIH. She quickly
became more than a doctor to us; she was a friend. She related
to kids so well, because she was in some ways like a kid herself.
Lisa knew how to talk to children, and she could be something
of a smart aleck. When I got to know her a little better, she
confided that she had been a sickly child, so she had another
level of understanding, too. The kids, including Hydeia, simply
adored her.

During her training at NIH, I happened to be up there, and
the two of us went out shopping. We hadn't planned to buy anything, but we found a beautiful coat that we both fell in love
with. It came in black and in olive green. Because Lisa and I
could wear each other's clothes, and we both wanted both coats,
we made a deal: She would buy one, and I would buy the other.
Whenever one of us wanted to wear the other color, we would
trade. That is the kind of friends we became. Later, when Lisa
and her partner wanted to adopt a child, Cindy, Diana, and I
helped out as much as we could. Having walked that road ourselves, we were able to guide her through the red tape and the
bureaucracy of adopting. In fact, I took care of one of her babies
while they waited for the final approval. Lisa and her partner
would visit my house as much as they could. Once that little
girl was adopted, I baby-sat. Lisa also baby-sat for Hydeia and
Keisha. Lisa's decision to make pediatric AIDS her career was a
godsend to us. We not only had a caring doctor who had been
trained by NIH, we also had a good friend.

While most people would jump at the chance to garner public recognition, I had learned that media attention could be a

double-edged sword. In the course of becoming a "face" of pe-diatric AIDS, Hydeia had raised awareness about the issues chil-dren like her face. That, of course, was a good thing. Over the years, many people have asked me if I ever had second thoughts about letting Hydeia go public, and I have to say no. She be-lieves in her mission, and I support her in it, as I would support any of my children in pursuing their dreams. At the same time, though, I learned early and quickly that just because the world comes knocking on your door, you don't necessarily always have to answer.

Because of Hydeia's association with NIH and the Pediatric AIDS Foundation, she has met many celebrities through the years. The most important work of an organization like the Pe-diatric AIDS Foundation is done by doctors, nurses, researchers, parents, and others whose names you may never know. Eliza-beth Glaser and other AIDS activists also realized, however, that without the attention and the funding that celebrities and high-profile people draw to your cause, little gets done. After all these years, I am still impressed by the time and energy I've seen celebrities devote to this issue, either by speaking publicly about it or by lending their names and their talents to fund-raising. I think I speak for everyone in this community when I say that we are all thankful for their help.

Fortunately, we have had many positive experiences with such celebrities. However, early on, there was one incident that forced me to step back and be more cautious about anyone who was interested in Hydeia. When Hydeia was about six years old, she got the opportunity to meet a certain celebrity. This woman offered to let her come to the set where she was shooting a new movie and spend the day. Hydeia could see the studio, have lunch with the star, and so on. It was a very generous gesture, and I thanked her but said I'd ask Hydeia first. Of course, Hy-deia was thrilled. Given the chance to meet this woman, I think most adults would have jumped.

When the big day arrived, Hydeia was very excited. From the

moment we entered the studio lot, we got the VIP treatment from everyone. Hydeia just beamed as the star talked to her, showed her around the movie set, and introduced her to everyone they encountered as "my friend Hydeia." She told Hydeia what "good friends" they were, how she could "always" call her, how they would see each other again, and so on. This would have been heady stuff for anyone, but for a child Hydeia's age, it was something else that even I didn't fully appreciate. To this woman, *friend* meant someone you like who happens to be there at the moment. To Hydeia, *friend* meant friend. By the time we left, I felt that we had been treated to a rare and pleasant time with someone we would probably never see or hear from again. Hydeia, however, believed that she had made a true friend.

During this period Hydeia was still having many health problems, and hospital stays that ran weeks were the norm. She would be lying in a hospital bed, burning up with fever and miserable, and yet be asking me, "When is my friend going to call me?" It is very hard to explain to a young child that adults don't always mean what they say, or that they don't always mean it as much as you wish they did. At first I tried to placate Hydeia by saying that maybe the famous woman was busy, or maybe she didn't have our number, or maybe she was traveling. Hydeia would be okay about it for a while, and then it would start right back up again. As a family, we had enough on our plate just living our lives without me feeling like I had to make excuses for some celebrity who never had any intention of being my daughter's friend. There were times when I felt like picking up the telephone and calling the famous person and saying, "Do you have any idea how my daughter feels about you? Do you realize that when you say you are her friend and you say you're going to call and you say that you really care about her, she fully expects you to follow up? Do you know what it feels like to have doctors telling me in one ear that my daughter may be in a serious health crisis and then in the other hearing her cry because she hasn't heard from her 'friend'? Do you know how stupid I feel making up excuses for someone who in this real world we live in does not even really exist?"

Of course, I never did. From then on, however, you can be sure that I viewed any celebrity interested in meeting Hydeia through different eyes. I know that I ruffled some feathers among personal assistants, managers, and public-relations reps. We were never as impressed with famous people as some people may have thought we should be, but I didn't care. From that moment on, when it came to anything dealing with media, celebrities, and publicity, I set the terms.

One of the more interesting—and enduring—relationships to evolve out of this celebrity hoopla was with Janet Jackson. It began a few years later, when Hydeia was about nine. Apparently, Janet saw some footage of Hydeia at one of the Pediatric AIDS Foundation's picnics. She contacted the PAF and asked for our number. When one of Elizabeth's partners called me to ask if it was okay to give it out, I said sure. It was summertime, just days before Hydeia's birthday, and we were planning her party at a local indoor amusement place, when the phone calls began. First it was Janet's personal assistant, then her agent, then someone else, then finally Rene Elizondo, who everyone thought was her boyfriend but to whom she was secretly married. To every person who called I said exactly the same thing: "I need to talk to Janet before she talks to or meets Hydeia. I don't want my daughter to get any false hopes about the type of relationship she will have with Janet. I need to be sure that Janet understands the full impact of what she says to Hydeia and is sensitive to the issues we have to deal with."

Naturally, everyone I spoke with tried desperately to reassure me that Janet was a good person, that she really cared, that she would never do anything that would harm Hydeia. And I'm sure, as I told them, that what they said was absolutely true. However—and after the second or third call, I was getting a little testy—I was her mother. Celebrity or no celebrity, I didn't care who you were. This was my daughter, these were my rules. Now, I knew that part of the problem was that celebrities and their people don't often hear the word *no* from people like me, because we're supposed to be so thrilled and flattered to have their attention. The idea that I was setting some conditions for the visit seemed to throw everyone for a loop.

By the time Rene called, I felt as if I'd explained myself enough, take it or leave it. He was an extremely kind, soft-spoken young man, and he seemed to understand what I was saying. When he said that Janet would like to come to meet Hydeia on her birthday, I said no. The party was already planned, and it was an event for Hydeia. I didn't want her to be upstaged on her special day by anyone, not even Janet. I thanked him and asked him to relay to Janet that while I did appreciate the gesture, we needed to work out another day. Then he said something interesting: that Hydeia was the first child Janet really wanted to meet. Usually if she saw a child who had a special need or problem, she would send them something. Hydeia, however, had touched her in a special way. That was fine, I said, but it still didn't change my terms.

It was Hydeia's birthday. For several days before, one delivery person after another had come bearing presents, so when a man rang the bell and asked, "Is this the Broadbent residence?" I assumed it was another package and said, "Yes."

"Is anyone else home?" he asked.

"Why?"

"I just need to know."

"Well, if you've got a big package to bring in, there is nobody here to help you, so you better get to hauling."

"Oh," he said. "Okay." Then, oddly, he walked toward the van, then stopped and stood a few feet from the door. He nodded toward the van, and the next thing I knew a slender guy and a small woman with reddish hair were walking toward the house. Curious, Hydeia had come to stand beside me. As the figures got closer, she said, "Mommy?"

"What?" I asked, distracted. These were the best-dressed and strangest-acting delivery people I'd ever seen.

"That's Janet Jackson," she said casually, the same way she would have said, "Oh, there's Daddy."

The young man approached. "Mrs. Broadbent, I'm Rene, and Janet wanted to meet Hydeia."

"Yes?" I replied, not too warmly.

Rene looked a little embarrassed. "I know you wanted to talk with Janet prior to her coming, but she was afraid you would say no." I looked over at Janet, who said nothing. "You know, she's very shy and she doesn't come across on the phone very well." His voice trailed off into silence.

"Hi," she offered, so softly I could barely hear her.

"I asked that you call me," I said to her. "I made it very clear to everyone in your organization I talked to—including Rene—that I needed to speak with you directly before you met Hydeia."

"I know," she replied. "But I feel better talking to you in person. I understand your concerns, and I would never do or say anything to hurt your daughter."

"I know you wouldn't do that deliberately, but I know from experience that people sometimes use phrases and words that have one meaning to them and an entirely different meaning to the child they're talking to. I don't want you telling Hydeia anything that you're not going to follow up with. I don't want you telling her that you're her friend or anything like that, because a friend is someone who is here, someone who comes when you need them, that you talk to whenever you feel like it, that you go and visit. Don't make Hydeia any promises you're not prepared to keep."

"I would never do that," she said.

Then I invited them in. Hydeia and Janet both speak so softly they had what I call "mumble conversations." If you weren't sitting right beside them, you would have no idea what they were talking about. Both Rene and Janet struck me as kind, sincere people, and at one point Janet told Hydeia she could sit on her lap.

"I don't want to sit on your lap, Janet, because my backpack will hurt your chest." She looked at me. "Won't it, Mommy?"

I smiled. "You don't care if it hurts my chest," I answered playfully.

She looked at Janet, then said, "Okay," and sat on her lap.

Janet and Rene stayed for most of the day. At one point, they took Hydeia out to the local Toys "R" Us for what turned into a major shopping spree. With Hydeia sitting in a shopping cart, Rene and Janet hit every aisle and stopped in front of every big-ticket item and asked, "Do you like this?" or "Do you like to do this?" Hydeia would say yes, never realizing that Rene was pocketing those tickets you bring to the cashier for items that are too large to put in your cart. It wasn't until after everything had been rung up and they started loading the van that Hydeia realized that she now owned a battery-powered jeep she could drive, a battery-powered motorcycle she could ride, a karaoke system, a small piano, a keyboard, a doll stroller—when all she had actually asked for was a doll. For most kids, this would be a fairy-tale moment, but when Hydeia heard the total— over two thousand dollars—she asked Janet, "Isn't this a lot of money to spend just on toys?" Even at that age, she would think of how much good that money could do spent in other ways.

Janet just replied, "No, it's not."

Before Janet left she told us about her apartment in Malibu and the dolphins you could see from the beach. She promised that one day she and Rene would have us out to visit them. As she spoke, I caught her eye and gave her a look that said, "Remember what I told you!" Rene must have seen it, too, because he added, "For real!" and repeated it a couple of times. As they were leaving, Rene gave me all of their phone numbers, including his personal cell number. We said good-bye, and I admit, I was impressed with them, but only time would tell if they were as "for real" as I thought.

So I was pleasantly surprised to get a call not more than a week later inviting Hydeia and me out to California. For the next couple of years, we saw quite a bit of Janet and Rene. We attended shows and rehearsals, and spent a weekend in Los Angeles as their guests during rehearsals for the *janet* tour. Janet phoned Hydeia often. Hydeia used to crack up Janet and Rene with her dead-on impersonation of Martin Lawrence's misguided fly girl character, Sheneneh Jenkins.

True to her word, Janet never misled Hydeia, never promised anything she didn't come through with. She became, in every sense of the word, a true friend. Unfortunately, Janet began to slip into the serious, long-term depression that she would later talk about after she released her *Velvet Rope* album. I remember once being backstage with Hydeia outside Janet's dressing room. Janet's parents, Katherine and Joseph Jackson, had just come out, and as we walked in, Hydeia saw Janet wiping away tears. Hydeia was always perceptive beyond her years, and she sensed that something was wrong. "Why was she crying?" Hydeia asked. I quickly concocted some explanation about how sometimes performers get very emotional before or after a show, but she looked me in the eye and said, "No, Mommy. She's sad." In the midst of her own health crises, Hydeia would be worrying. "I hope Janet is okay," she would say, or "I wonder why Janet is so sad." Understandably, we heard from Janet less often, and whatever overtures she did make, I didn't go out of my way to encourage. Hydeia was prepared to be a friend, but as a child. She couldn't help but get caught up in being worried about Janet, which wasn't Janet's fault but was not appropriate for a child. I allowed the relationship to lapse, though I think Janet knows that she would always be welcome in Hydeia's life again.

_____

Later in 1992, when Hydeia was about eight, the television news program *20/20* wanted to profile Hydeia for a piece on pediatric AIDS and specifically the research being done by NIH. I agreed to it, on one condition—that they also cover the opening of the Reach Out center. After working on it for so long and already receiving the Pediatric AIDS Foundation A Time for Heroes Award for our efforts, we were finally ready to open our doors. Even though it was a "local" story, we thought it was important to get out the word that you don't have to be a major institution like NIH or a big foundation to have a major impact on these children and their families. At first the producers balked, but I stood firm: No Reach Out, no Hydeia.

The *20/20* crew began filming for the piece, traveling first to NIH, where they interviewed Dr. Pizzo and showed Hydeia on the playground at the Children's Inn. In Las Vegas they filmed an often aired piece showing Hydeia getting ready for bed, with the TPN tubes, the Hickman, and the backpack. There must have been something about seeing Hydeia in the little mesh T-shirt she wore to hold the TPN tubes in place (she is extremely allergic to tape), because that minute or so of footage has aired on so many other programs she's appeared on since. At that time she was all puffed up because of the corticosteroids. Yet she was smiling happily and talking nonchalantly as she walked with reporter Tom Jarriel through a sterile room at Las Vegas's Wellness Clinic (NIH would not permit filming in its hospital), where they draw blood. The only time she became upset was when talking about her friend Dougie, who had recently died. In the introduction to the piece, host Hugh Downs described Hydeia as "a little girl as unique as her name." Singing on the swings in front of Reach Out or charming everyone with her imitation of Ray Charles, Hydeia made it all look so easy.

For me, though, the process was much, much harder. All these years later, I still have trouble thinking back to the day that Hydeia coded, so you can imagine how raw my feelings were back then, only months later. I know that the producers and crew would have loved to catch me crying, but I refused to let that happen. In fact, I even told Tom, "I will tell you this story, but I may get emotional, and you had better turn the cameras off. I don't want to see one tear when this airs." I talked about her coding, but I asked them to film me from the back, so you couldn't see my face if I started to cry. They showed some footage of Hydeia and Tyler's wedding, and in telling the story of how it came about, I said, "Is all that wisdom there because you're getting ready to really utilize it? As you get older, is it going to get better? Or is it all just crammed into that little body because you aren't going to be there very long?" This is a question that may never be answered.

To give a fuller picture of Hydeia's life, the *20/20* crew staged a visit to Dr. Lisa's office. Timing-wise, they had just missed a real visit by days, so we went through the motions of a routine checkup: Dr. Lisa listening to her chest, making a funny remark, looking in her throat and her ears. With Hydeia, however, nothing was ever routine. In the course of this "pretend" exam, Dr. Lisa announced to me that the new rash on Hydeia's torso was herpes. I can be heard exclaiming, "You've got to be kidding!" Of course, it was always possible that Hydeia could have anything, literally, so I shouldn't have been surprised. Still, there was something bizarrely ironic about it all. We couldn't even pretend to go to the doctor without something new cropping up!

Hydeia's and Patricia's doctors knew my attitude toward taking precautions to avoid HIV infection. I was careful whenever I felt that there was what I considered a real risk. However, early on I had decided not to wear latex gloves when handling hypodermic needles. I know of course that the universal safety precautions call for wearing them. But I never felt that my grip on the syringe was secure enough when I was wearing gloves. Since the greatest exposure risk was from an accidental needle stick, and since a needle would go right through latex, I felt that I had less of a chance of getting stuck if I had a better hold on the syringe. I wouldn't recommend this to everyone, of course. In our home we had a sharps box—a red sealed plastic container with a special opening that allows you to place the entire used needle and syringe inside without touching other debris. You couldn't open it; once you placed a needle in, it couldn't come out. Once it was full, the home health care people would take it to be safely and properly destroyed.

Dr. Lisa was constantly reminding me about taking all the precautions. Knowing that I didn't wear gloves, she would say, "Be careful with your needles and your sharps box." During our last couple of visits, I noticed that Lisa looked tired. She and her partner, Annie, had taken in three children, and taking care of her patients with HIV/AIDS meant that she was on call virtually round the clock. Still, she looked unusually run-down to a degree that a hectic schedule alone didn't quite explain. One day after a routine visit with Hydeia, she asked if we could talk privately in her office. She started telling me about a new doctor who was coming, who would work with Hydeia and the other kids. I didn't quite understand what she meant until she said, "Pat, I got stuck."

I was speechless. Looking across the desk, I could see her eyes welling up with tears, though she struggled to keep it together. She was in the office late one night in May and picked up a needle she found lying on the floor. As she put it into the sharps container, the needle pricked her finger. Inexplicably, Lisa began to show symptoms of the virus almost immediately, and her doctor advised her that if she did not give up her practice, he would no longer treat her. It was that bad. Almost instinctively, I slipped off my Until There's a Cure bracelet and handed it to her. The cuff bracelet bearing a small raised AIDS ribbon had been the idea of two mothers of children with AIDS. Once you put it on, you were to wear it until there was a cure. Lisa looked at it, then placed it on her wrist and said, "Please don't tell anyone. I want to keep this private."

"Have you talked to anyone?" I asked. Only a few people, she said. "How about Linda Lewis?" Linda was a doctor at NIH who had worked with Lisa while she trained there. They had become good friends, and I thought Linda could help. Lisa shook her head. I sat there feeling stunned, shocked, saddened, and totally responsible. It would be years before I could honestly tell myself that I wasn't at least partly to blame for what happened. After all, if Diana, Cindy, and I had not pursued Dr. Lisa, if we had not arranged for her to go to NIH for training, if, if, if—I could go on forever. I thought about her partner, Annie, and their children. Every case of HIV infection is terrible and sad, of course. Yet Lisa's situation was all the more poignant. In all these years, I have never come across a single parent, doctor, health care worker, family member, or anyone who has been stuck. Though the risk is theoretically always there, the odds of it happening are in fact minuscule. Although part of my mind realized that this was completely irrational, I couldn't help but think that Dr. Lisa was going to die because she cared so much about our kids. I couldn't stop myself from wondering how much better her life would be today if she had never met me, if she had never accepted this challenge.

I didn't plan to tell anyone until Cindy phoned to say that Dr. Lisa had told her a couple of days before me. After a lot of thought, I broke my promise to Lisa and phoned Dr. Linda Lewis at NIH. I explained the situation to her and asked that she call Lisa, which she did. Although I knew that Lisa might not be pleased that I told Linda, having Linda to talk with turned out to be a very good thing for her. She really did need that. I was also concerned because considering the short amount of time since Lisa had been exposed, her health was deteriorating rapidly. She came to Hydeia's ninth birthday party (she had also been at Hydeia and Tyler's wedding), and within just weeks she was having trouble walking.

When Hydeia heard the news, she was very sad. She loved Dr. Lisa and was concerned about her. In an odd way, their roles reversed, with Hydeia becoming something of a doctor herself as she told Lisa, "You're going to be okay, Dr. Lisa." Hydeia also made sure to remind me, "You know, Dr. Lisa is always telling you to be careful with the needles and my Hickman." Hydeia had seen so many people pass by then, I think she could see Lisa losing ground. Still, she never let Lisa give up hope. Hydeia and Lisa gave a talk together at a local college.

Lisa's disease progressed rapidly. She contracted cryptosporidium, a protozoa that attacks the intestinal tract and often produces violent, almost untreatable diarrhea in immune-compromised people. One day Annie called me to say that Lisa was nearing the end. Would I like to come and see her? I asked to speak with her on the telephone instead. The last thing Lisa said to me was, "I know that this is devastating. If you don't want to come over, I know you love me. I know that I am in your heart." A day or so later, she passed.

Every passing leaves its mark, yet Lisa's was somehow different. Not long after she died, I had a dream that felt too real to be a dream. Lisa was standing at the foot of my bed, holding her—or should I say, our?—coat. "Pat, I wanted to let you know that you have to let Hydeia talk. You know you're not exploiting her, and I know you're not exploiting this situation." Surprised as I was to see Lisa standing there, what she said didn't surprise me. As Hydeia became better known, I had often talked with Lisa about how public she should be and where to draw the line. "Here," she said, offering me her coat, "I brought this to you because I know you need both of them." Then she smiled and disappeared.

A few days later Annie called. I asked her how she and the kids were doing, and we talked a little. Then Annie said, "I have something for you from Lisa. Do you know what she left you?"

I smiled. "I think I know," I replied, then told her about the dream.

"Pat, Lisa is everywhere," Annie said. And I think that she was. Lisa's work was widely recognized within the AIDS community. Clark County's Meals on Wheels program for people with HIV/AIDS was named Dr. B.'s Kitchen in her memory.

It was a time of many changes for our family. We moved from the house Hydeia had known all her life to a smaller place that Loren and I had bought as a rental property. By then Loren and I had separated, so it was me and the girls—Keisha, Hydeia, and Patricia. Even though Hydeia's and Patricia's medical expenses were covered by NIH and Medicaid, the fact that I had not worked in a few years—and may never be able to work again—forced us to make significant changes in our lifestyle. As attached as I thought I was to my other home, dealing with Hydeia and Patricia had forced a different perspective onto many things.

After so many years of living my life around AIDS, I remember being speechless when someone once asked me what I would do if I had time to myself. It had been so long since I'd had an hour that was not held hostage to my children's illness, I honestly didn't know what to say. I had forgotten what that felt like, and I had somehow learned to stop thinking about it. The move to the smaller house was symbolic of the changes we had weathered over the past five or six years. What I noticed more were the little details of my old life, the old me that disappeared under the shadow of AIDS. For my first four children I kept photo albums, into which I religiously placed snapshots of every major family event. Today, years' worth of photos have accumulated in disorganized piles around the house. It's a small thing, but a reminder that the time I once thought I controlled is no longer mine.

Over the years I had kept a journal detailing every medication, fever, symptom, procedure, conversation with a doctor. By then Hydeia had been on AZT for a while and things were going well. I hadn't thought much about the black ledger book for a couple of years. I'm not superstitious, but I couldn't bring myself to throw it away. One day I happened to find it in the dining room buffet, and as I started reading it, a terrible feeling came over me. It wasn't that I had forgotten everything Hydeia had been through, but I had managed to put the fear of that time away somewhere. Opening the book was like being drawn into a nightmare. My heart began to flutter, and I could feel the tension tighten my neck as I read: "Nocardia, 4 mls. of this; four mls. of that, ten days. Fever: 106. Just in the hospital. Admitted Wednesday, changed TPN formula . . ." Four years of worry and wonder, hope and despair, summed up in dosages, schedules, and notes, took me back to that place.

I felt myself grieving, which in a way, I suppose, didn't make sense. After all, Hydeia was still here; those bad days were behind us, at least for now. While I would never lose sight of what Hydeia had gained and the gift of time and life she had been given, I could not ignore countless losses she had endured to get to this point. Reading the journal reminded me of how much I had forgotten—or forced myself to forget. I also realized that everything the notebook contained was now totally irrelevant; it meant nothing today. It was just a ghost from the past that I couldn't ignore, and it made me realize how much I'd disconnected from myself emotionally. It frightened me to realize that I'd gotten through that time without really knowing where I was going. Then I didn't know enough; I hadn't seen enough to do anything but move forward on a sort of blind faith. Knowing what I know now, I wondered, would I be able to rise to the challenge again? Would I have it within me to be the woman who wrote that ledger if I had to do it again today?

I don't know how long I was reading before I decided to throw the book away. I took it outside, tossed it in the garbage can, came back in the house, and lit a cigarette. That's over, I kept telling myself. It's gone.

At nine, Hydeia was far from grown-up, but she was no longer truly a child. She knew about as much about AIDS and her medical situation as anyone. She had been drawing her own blood, giving herself shots, cleaning her own Hickman, and being responsible for many of her daily routines for a few years. As a patient, Hydeia had been exceptional. I knew, however, from other parents I'd seen that as children with chronic health problems get older, they sometimes rebel against the regimens and restrictions.

By then Hydeia had been receiving medication on a continuous intravenous infusion from the little pump in her backpack for nearly three years. Dr. Pizzo thought that since she was eating better and her health was very good, it might be a good idea to try oral meds. If she could get the same benefits from oral AZT as from the intravenous form, we could eliminate the backpack. Not only would it be more convenient, but also we could dispense with the daily routine of cleaning the Hickman and eliminate one other source of potentially serious infection or other complication.

By then Hydeia knew everything about the pump and the Hickman that I did. She could prime the pump, straighten the lines, change her meds, and flush the line, as well as perform the intricate, time-consuming tasks required to maintain her Hickman. I always watched her, of course, but she was a pro. You would think she would be happy to be free of it, but once the pump and backpack were removed, Hydeia felt so uncomfortable, she continued wearing them for several days before finally giving them up. I guess it was a security issue; they had been a part of her for so long. It took only a few days, however, before Hydeia began to appreciate the freedom of not wearing the pump. She could suddenly do things she hadn't done in years, like sit on my lap and really lean back against me, go swimming without having to disconnect the pump and close the Hickman every time she went into the pool, then resterilize the Hickman and reconnect the pump every time she got out. She could get up to use the bathroom in the middle of the night without carrying the pump. She could lie on her back. She was too young when she first got the pump to appreciate how restrictive it was. Once she got a taste of life without the backpack, though, there was no turning back.

After a few weeks on oral AZT, Dr. Mueller at NIH gave us some bad news: Hydeia's body was not absorbing enough of it; she would have to go back on the pump. Hydeia understood why she needed the pump, but she was adamant. "It hurts my back, it's too heavy, I have to carry it all the time." Hydeia's list of arguments went on and on. I could have forced her to do it, and Dr. Mueller had wanted to put it back on right away. I thought it would be better if Hydeia came around to deciding to wear the pump herself. It was clear that Hydeia had to go back on the intravenous AZT the next day. Every day that she was not maintaining an adequate level of AZT in her system, the virus was replicating and invading new cells.

At dinner, we talked about the backpack. "You know if you don't put the backpack on, you're going to start getting sick again. You've been doing really well. Do you want to start spending a lot of time in the hospital and being sick again because you don't want the backpack?"

"It hurts my back," she said. "And if I sit on your lap, I can't lean back, because the backpack will stick you in the chest."

"I know, and it is uncomfortable for me sometimes. But I can manage it."

Hydeia looked me straight in the eye and said, "I'm not going to put it on."

Now, there are parents who believe that a child with a chronic or terminal illness has enough problems without being made unhappy by Mom or Dad. When you don't know how much time your child has on this earth, it's very tempting to let things slide, let her have her way, and avoid the confrontations, the harsh words, and the hurt feelings. At the same time, it's very important that you not let your child's disease stop you from being the parent. And being the parent means being the boss. It also means sometimes delivering the hard news, the reality check.

When Hydeia said she wasn't putting the backpack on, I said, "Okay. However, the bottom line is, if you don't wear the backpack, you are saying that you want to be sick. If you don't wear the backpack, you're going to have to go into the hospital. Now I have Patricia and Keisha. I may not be able to spend all the time at the hospital with you. If you decide to be sick, you're going to have to do the hospital time by yourself."

Hydeia walked away. I was doing the dishes later when she came in and said, "Mommy, I don't want to get sick. I'll let Dr. Mueller put the backpack back on me."

"I think that's a smart choice," I replied, the whole time thanking God that we didn't have to force her to do something she didn't want to do.

Although Hydeia was still very small for her age, there was no doubt that she was growing up. That summer she went to camp for the first time, at Camp Dream Street, for children who are medically fragile with blood disorders. Hydeia was one of the first children with AIDS to attend Dream Street.

Camp Dream Street was not a woodsy place but a country-club-type setting in Silver Springs, California, about a six-hour drive from our home. Hydeia, Cindy, Tyler, and I drove up. After we got her stuff into her room and gave her meds to the camp nurse, we had lunch together. She was happy to be there and seemed to be looking forward to her first camp experience. Tyler would be there, too, and he had gone the year before, so she had someone there who knew the ropes. Toward the end of lunch, a buzzer rang, the signal that it was time for parents to leave. Although I knew intellectually that I wasn't going to stay there with her, the realization didn't really hit me until then. Hydeia looked up at me, and I put on my happy-mommy face and said, "Okay now, you have a good week, and I'll be back to pick you up on Sunday."

She looked at me as if she didn't know what I was talking about. "What's the matter?" I asked.

"You're not staying?"

"No, this is camp for just kids."

"Suppose I get sick?"

"I don't think you will," I answered, all the while knowing that I had asked myself the same question. "But if you do get sick, Hydeia, they'll take you to the hospital, and I can fly up here in about forty-five minutes. I will be here." I looked into her eyes. "I will come."

Hydeia just looked at me. She wasn't about to cry, but she had a dubious expression and needed reassurance. "Hydeia, if I thought you would get sick, I wouldn't leave you." We hugged and said our good-byes, but the whole trip home I must have driven Cindy crazy. I didn't feel comfortable. How did I know the staff would know what to do? If Hydeia decided she didn't want to go with the program, she wasn't going to go.

Between the drive to the camp and back, it was a very long day, and I arrived home exhausted. For all the times we had spent together and all the moments I had wished that she could be healthy enough to be away from me for even a day or so, I realized how much I missed her. To see her belongings throughout the house and not have her there was like reliving a long-forgotten nightmare. I remember telling Loren, "This is what it would be like if Hydeia died." Of course, I knew she was away, at camp, in safe hands. I knew she was coming home later that week. I knew things were okay. Still, my mind kept wandering back to the same idea—that this was what it would be like if, when. I knew that AIDS had made Hydeia extremely dependent on me. What I hadn't realized was how it had also made me dependent on her. I needed to see her to know she was okay.

I became so upset over this, I called Lori at NIH and said, "I think I want to go and get her." Lori convinced me that what I felt was perfectly normal and that Hydeia did need opportunities to be independent, or at least without her mother at her side round the clock. After a day or so passed with no word from the camp, I phoned and discovered that she was doing great. Well, except for arguing with the nurses that she could take care of her own pump and Hickman and meds, thank you. When I heard that, I knew she'd do just fine.

SIX

Fortunately, Hydeia's run of good health continued for the next couple of years. She began doing more speaking engagements, and in the years since, she has shared her message with organizations, universities, schools, churches, and corporations across the country. On one of our first trips, we went to Fort Lauderdale, Florida, at the request of a woman whose grown son has since died of AIDS. She had formed an organization to provide affordable housing to people with HIV/AIDS, and Hydeia was the keynote speaker at their first major fund-raiser. A newspaper reporter met us at the airport and asked Hydeia why she was coming to Florida to speak.

Now, you have to picture this little girl, then about seven but the size of a four-year-old, looking this reporter in the eye and saying, "I came to Florida because I have friends who live here and they can't tell anybody that they have AIDS. So I came down here to talk with people so that these ignorant people can understand that you can't get AIDS by being a friend."

"Well, how do you know it's like that down here?" the reporter asked skeptically.

"I have friends that live here," Hydeia replied simply. And that's how it was for Hydeia.

The fund-raiser was a big success—more than two hundred people heard her speak at the Sun Sentinel Center—and we were happy to have been part of it. As far as I knew, Hydeia had volunteered her time to a cause she believed in. A few days later, the woman sent us a very gracious thank-you note, and inside was a check. It was the first time Hydeia had received money for speaking. I remember thinking that this proved what I'd always believed to be true: God watches over babies and fools.

Around this time, Hydeia had begun attending Camp Heartland, a wonderful place for children with HIV and for those who are affected by it (such as siblings). In 1991 a twenty-year-old college senior named Neil Willenson read a story about a kindergartner with AIDS who was being ostracized by the community. Neil befriended the little boy and his family. When the boy said that all he wanted to do was go to camp like other kids, Neil found his mission. In 1993 he founded Camp Heartland at a rented camp facility in Wisconsin. For the next few years, he would rent camps in different places, and in 1998 Camp Heartland found a permanent home on eighty wooded acres in Minnesota. Today Neil and Camp Heartland are so well known and respected that in spring 2001 *People* magazine named Neil one of the world's most eligible bachelors. Who says good deeds don't pay?

Being at Camp Heartland was wonderful for Hydeia, and she made many new friends. For a few years she toured the country speaking out about AIDS with Neil and some other Heartland campers as part of the Journey of Hope. She would introduce herself by saying, "My name is Hydeia L. Broadbent, and I am a singer, a dancer . . . and I have AIDS." She made the audience chuckle with her boast that, thanks to the damage to her nose cartilage, she could blow bigger boogers than anyone else.

No matter where she was, though, she could not stop advo-

TEN YEARS LATER
WHAT I WANT THE WORLD TO KNOW

It's been 10 years that I've been living with AIDS. It hasn't been real hard. I haven't been sick for almost two years. That's nice. When you are sick you probably feel real lousy. Rest, good medicines and lots of love helps.

I want the world to know that it has been very good for me and no one needs to be afraid of me.

Hydeia
Age nine

cating. While this was admirable, some of Hydeia's ideas about what it meant to have HIV/AIDS were not the same as other people's. When it came to questions of being honest and out about having HIV/AIDS, the decisions that our family made for Hydeia were not the same another family might make. Do I believe that we did the right thing? Absolutely. For us, the issues have always been, as I like to say, cut-and-dried. My goals for Hydeia in terms of self-acceptance, self-esteem, and openness were always nonnegotiable. Through my years in social work and talking with so many parents up at NIH, though, I knew when to turn it on and when to turn it off. I figured out who wanted to hear what I had to say and who didn't. But I am an adult. Hydeia, on the other hand, is a child and an advocate, and those two parts of her are inseparable.

Because of the way she has been raised, Hydeia has always been especially sensitive about the issue of disclosure. The idea of a child having to hide a diagnosis has always struck her as a major wrong. At Camp Heartland she ran into a little boy she knew from NIH. I had gotten to know his mother a little bit, and we knew he was from a small town in Louisiana where the family felt compelled to hide his illness. After he told her what it was like for him and why he couldn't tell anyone, she said, "I wouldn't hide. Why would you hide? Is something wrong with you? There's nothing wrong with you. If I was you, when I went home, I would just tell them, 'Yeah, I got AIDS, and you can't catch it, so get over it!' "

Whatever else Hydeia said, it made an impression, because the little boy went home to Louisiana and informed his mother that he was going to tell the kids at school that he had AIDS. His mother called me, very concerned. She knew who Hydeia was, and she understood why she had said what she said to her son. However, she wanted me to understand the reality of her situation. They lived in a small, rural town where the only person known to have had AIDS was a gay man whom the community had run out of town. She asked if Hydeia and I would come to her town and speak to the people. When I told her that I would be willing to, but we didn't have the money to do that, she said, "Oh, I thought you had a foundation."

"No, we don't," I answered, realizing that the idea of starting one had never crossed my mind.

"Well, then maybe she needs to stop telling kids to do this," the mother said.

"That's impossible. I may have raised Hydeia to see things a certain way, but I do not control what she thinks or what she says," I said. "I believe that if you tell people and act like you're scared, then you're going to have problems. It's like you're asking someone for permission to be accepted. I don't leave myself or Hydeia open for anyone to doubt what we want to do. If there's doubting to be done, we make sure that we are so straightforward and confident in our right to be wherever we want to be, they end up doubting themselves. What you need to do if he does decide to tell is take control of the situation yourself. Go to the newspaper, tell the people at school, and get it over with all at once. Explain that he's a hemophiliac and that he was infected by Factor VIII. He's not the only hemophiliac in your area. You know there must be other people, too. Get people's attention off the idea of HIV and convince them to put themselves in your place and in your son's place. Make them think about how they would want to be treated if they were in your shoes. Remind them that they shouldn't be focusing on your son; they should be focusing on how they can help."

The mother was understandably a little resistant, but she went ahead and let her son tell. The world did not end, and the sky didn't fall. And this little boy could finally live his life out from under the shadows and the lies.

I realized then that it would be impossible for Hydeia to accept all the invitations to speak that she wanted to if we had to fund the expenses out of our limited personal income. The idea of starting a foundation never crossed my mind until after *20/20* aired. I was contacted by a woman from Montgomery, Alabama, named Claire Milligan. She told me that although she had never heard of there being any children with AIDS in Montgomery, she assumed that there were, and she wanted to help. She wanted to start a foundation to raise AIDS awareness and asked if she could name it in Hydeia's honor. I said yes, and the Hydeia L. Broadbent Foundation began. A couple of years later, Claire called to ask if I would like to take over the foundation, since family obligations made it difficult for her to continue running it. Halfheartedly, I did, all the while knowing that I had neither the time nor the energy to run a nonprofit. At that point, I brought in Delores Bullard as executive director, and we put together a board of directors that includes my friends the Reverend Dr. Barbara King, Delores's husband, Conrad Bullard, and the Reverend O. C. Smith (yes, the O. C. Smith of "Little Green Apples" fame). As it exists today, the Hydeia L. Broadbent Foundation works to raise awareness and provide education about HIV/AIDS. Donations to the foundation, which come primarily from Hydeia's speaking fees, cover the costs of developing educational materials and programs. Hydeia's campaign to raise awareness has taken her everyplace from churches and rural schools to the Las Vegas stage.

Through a board member of Reach Out, Hydeia met singer Engelbert Humperdinck. Uncle Bert, as she soon began calling him, was one of those rare celebrities who not only supported the cause but actually did become a friend. Whenever he was in Las Vegas, he invited Hydeia to his show, and before long, she also became part of the show, joining him onstage and singing. She liked to heckle him playfully from the audience by calling out the punch lines to his stage patter.

Around this time, Hydeia also got to meet country singer Billy

Ray Cyrus. Then most famous for his hit "Achy Breaky Heart," Billy proved to be a sincere, sweet, and caring man. He would invite Hydeia onstage with him, and after meeting her, he agreed to do several AIDS benefit concerts, including Nashville Cares. There she sang a song she had written for her friends entitled "World, World, World."

> World, world, world—a loving world.
> Bluebirds flying, making a rainbow,
> Hummingbirds humming my favorite song.
> World, world, world—a loving world.
> Reach out and hold the children's hands,
> Pray, pray, pray, and maybe someday
> God will make a Band-Aid for the world,
> And maybe someday
> There will be no AIDS.

Billy Ray invited us to visit him at his home on the outskirts of Nashville. He and his wife, Tish, were very gracious, and I remember Billy being so shy that when he sang for us in his den, he had to turn his back. He was an interesting man; he had a real animal-hide tepee on his property. Hydeia liked Billy so much that she once turned down a request to appear with President Bill Clinton at the White House for World AIDS Day because she had already promised to be in Nashville with Billy. When Billy heard that she had refused the president's invitation, he couldn't believe it.

Early one morning I was awakened by the phone ringing.

"Mrs. Patricia Broadbent?"

"Yes?" I answered sleepily. "Who is this?"

The man on the phone identified himself as being from a car dealership somewhere in the Midwest, then said, "Your van is ready. When can we bring it out to Las Vegas?"

"I don't know anything about a van," I said irritably.

He started to explain, but I hung up. *Who is this fool?* I thought. Minutes later, the phone rang again. "Please don't hang up!" the poor man pleaded. "Are you Patricia Broadbent of . . ." and then he read off my address. When I confirmed it, he said, "Ma'am, I have your van here and ready to deliver."

"But I didn't order a van," I said. "I have no idea what you're talking about."

"Well, someone bought one for you," he replied.

"Who?"

"Well, I'm really not supposed to tell you," he said.

"Well, if you don't tell me, then you can't deliver it," I answered, still not convinced that this wasn't a prank call.

After going back and forth a couple of times, he finally relented: A Mr. Cyrus bought the van for us. I thought I'd drop the phone. In all the time we'd known Billy, we had never talked about my car. He noticed that it was getting old and took it upon himself to help. He never made a big deal about it, and he accepted our thanks graciously.

Hydeia was becoming a public figure in her own right, with all the hassles and the perks that entails. Ever since the piece ran on *20/20*, Hydeia has been approached by strangers who recognize her or, at least, feel certain they have seen her someplace before. People have been extremely kind, for the most part, but it can be difficult to run for the plane that's waiting when the guard at the security check insists on getting a picture. Every birthday and every Christmas brings a parade of deliveries— cards, letters, gifts, some from celebrities, others from regular people. Once Hydeia has opened and sorted through the gifts, we donate the duplicates to organizations for children.

It never occurred to me to be nervous about Hydeia becoming so well known until one night when she was onstage in Nashville with Billy Ray Cyrus. People crowding around the edge of the stage were calling out Hydeia's name and holding up teddy bears and cards. Naturally, Hydeia started to walk toward them when one of Billy's bodyguards yelled out, "Hydeia! Stop!" She spun around, scared to death, and looked at me. Not entirely clear what the problem was, I gestured for her to step back and walk toward the wings, where I was standing next to the bodyguard. She looked so scared, I reassured her that she hadn't done anything wrong. Then Billy's bodyguard said, "Baby, you can't get too close to people, because they might snatch you off the stage." Until that moment, it had never occurred to me that I had to add kidnapping to the list of bad things that might happen to my daughter. But on reflection, I realized the bodyguard was right. People can do crazy things.

When Hydeia was about nine, she was hospitalized briefly in Las Vegas. She shared a semiprivate room with a teenage girl, and the two of them got to know each other a little. One night both I and the girl's mother were there, and the girls were watching television when a commercial for the *National Enquirer* came on. Suddenly the screen filled with a picture of Billy Ray Cyrus and Hydeia, as the voice-over referred to her as "the little girl with AIDS." I was surprised to see it, because I had never spoken with anyone from the tabloid or given anyone permission to print a photograph of Hydeia. As I soon learned, however, she had officially become a public figure, so I had no control over these things. There was nothing negative or wrong about the *Enquirer* piece. Still, it was strange to see my daughter's face shining down from the television as she lay there in bed.

"That's you!" the girl in the next bed exclaimed as her mother glared at me.

"Yeah," I said, determined to keep cool.

"You got AIDS?" she asked Hydeia.

"Yeah," Hydeia replied calmly.

"Oh!" the girl yelped, panicking. "And I used the bathroom!"

I said nothing. Hydeia fixed her with a look and calmly said, "You cannot get AIDS from using a bathroom."

"But—" the mother started in a worried tone. Hydeia picked up on it right away.

"You can't get AIDS from sharing a room with me," Hydeia said to the girl. Then she looked at the mother and said, "You don't know how you can get AIDS? Maybe you'd better learn, so you can teach her what she should be doing and what she shouldn't be doing."

Instead of being offended or upset, the two of them listened while Hydeia did her thing, and all seemed well. The situation didn't bother Hydeia because she'd faced it so many times before. Even up at NIH, there were cancer patients (they were on the same floor as the kids with AIDS) who had a problem sharing a room with someone with AIDS. It's interesting that adults who have no problem being around someone with AIDS get nervous at the prospect of a child being around a child who has AIDS. I try to picture what they think kids do that's so different from what adults do in a normal, nonsexual relationship. I also wonder if that girl and her mother would have listened so politely and been so accepting if the child with AIDS in the next bed had not been on the TV or in the press.

Since that time, Hydeia has received many offers to do all kinds of things to promote herself. We always make sure that whatever she participates in or lends her name to is about AIDS awareness and education. Over the years we have declined many invitations and offers—some quite lucrative—because they would have promoted Hydeia as a personality instead of educating people about AIDS. It might seem that simply being famous is the way to get people to listen to you, but you can be famous for many things, and not all of them enhance your credibility. I always felt that Hydeia's secret weapon, the reason adults and college kids listened to her, was that she was real. Though her speeches kept to the same basic outline, I never knew exactly what she was going to say. No matter how many times I've seen her speak, I still marvel at how she does it.

She may present the same facts or use the same audience-participation activity she did a week or two before, but as long as I can see in her face that this is still new to her, too, we can continue. The first time I ever get the sense that she's just going through the motions, I've told her, we can stop. All these years later, even as the traveling has become so routine, once she hits that stage or someone puts a microphone in front of her, she's off and running. As long as there is someone who needs to learn about AIDS, Hydeia has something to say.

In June 1994 we flew out to Los Angeles for the annual A Time for Heroes picnic to benefit the Pediatric AIDS Foundation. If I have said it before, forgive me; were it not for Elizabeth Glaser and the PAF, I know that Hydeia would not be here today. So it was with great sadness that we began to realize that Elizabeth was losing her fight. She had lived for fourteen years with the virus, which at that time was extraordinary. Still, it wasn't long enough. It's never long enough.

By this time, we had a little routine for the event. Hydeia would speak with Elizabeth at the press conference, and then at the picnic itself Hydeia and Elizabeth would dance. This year, though, was different. Elizabeth was noticeably thinner and weaker, and so she sat on the ground with Hydeia resting between her legs. The two of them just talked. I remember Hydeia giving Elizabeth advice on what kind of port to get; Hydeia knew the pros and cons of each type. Elizabeth was Hydeia's hero, and at that year's press conference, Elizabeth said Hydeia was her inspiration. She mentioned how Hydeia was when they first met, how she had attended the first couple of picnics in a wheelchair because she was so weak. And now here she was, so healthy and full of life.

After we left that year, Hydeia was always asking to call Elizabeth. I had become good friends with Susan DeLaurentis and

Susie Zeegan, the other two cofounders of the foundation, and we kept in touch. Elizabeth couldn't speak and was confined to her bed. In late November Susie told me that things weren't looking good for Elizabeth. All I said to Hydeia was, "Elizabeth is not doing well." And she answered, "Okay, we'll call her tomorrow."

Unfortunately, all of those tomorrows ended on December 3, 1994, when Elizabeth passed away. Susan phoned me so that I could talk with Hydeia before she heard it on the news. I called Hydeia into my room and told her that Elizabeth had died. She looked at me, burst into tears, and said, "I knew that she was going to." We cried together. Hydeia vowed she would never attend another picnic, and I just let her talk. Like most people with AIDS, Elizabeth had suffered tremendously before she passed. For all the death that was around Hydeia, I know that thinking of it in terms of the end of suffering helped her.

I thought back to the first time I saw Elizabeth at the pediatric AIDS conference. She was the first person I'd ever met who was determined not to let this disease run her life, despite the fact that in almost every way, you could say that it had ruined it. Not only had Elizabeth fought to make AIDS drugs available to children, she was also the driving force behind the research demonstrating that a prenatal course of anti-HIV drugs could drastically reduce the chances of an HIV-positive mother passing the virus on to her unborn child. Named the Ariel Project, it has saved millions of lives.

Later we drove to Malibu for Elizabeth's memorial service. Her son, Jake, played the piano, and at the end we released balloons and watched them float up to heaven. It was a beautiful day, a chance to reflect on all that Elizabeth had given us. There was no question but that Paul Michael Glaser and Susan and Susie would carry on the fight. Elizabeth had dedicated her life to preserving the memory of her daughter and saving the life of her son. Her beautiful book, *In the Absence of Angels*, came out in 1991, just a few years before she passed. In her last chapter, she writes of walking Jake to school for his first day of kindergarten. "Jake was almost six," she writes, "and hope was still ours." Thanks to Elizabeth, that hope still is. As I write this, Jake is seventeen, and the Pediatric AIDS Foundation has grown to encompass children around the world.

The following June, Hydeia was reluctant to attend the picnic. She had mentioned several times that she could never go back again because she missed Elizabeth so much. But I would always remind her that even though Elizabeth had led the charge, she was counting on each and every one of us to continue. We went, and Hydeia found it very difficult to get through the usual press conference. It was one of the rare times she actually lost control in public, and she would turn to Susan or Susie and say, "I miss Elizabeth so much." She read a poem in which she wrote to Elizabeth, "One day, we will all be together, it is just not my time yet." Hydeia has come to see that by continuing Elizabeth's mission through her work, a part of Elizabeth is always with her. And that work was far from finished. When Elizabeth passed, she joined over 288,000 Americans who had died from AIDS.

In many ways 1995 was a watershed year in the history of AIDS. Thanks to political pressure from various AIDS groups, the federal government and the FDA in particular were finally shortening the approval process for new drugs. The pros of this were obvious: quicker access to potentially lifesaving drugs. While there was much to applaud in that, those of us who lived with AIDS knew all too well that the rapid-approval process had its downside, too. For one thing, with some drugs being approved as quickly as six months (compared with the usual three years or more), researchers did not always get to see the full range of side effects that might develop over time. The potential risks to patients were no longer confined to the strictly controlled protocol environments like NIH. Suddenly every patient was a test subject, assuming risks that most of us would opt to avoid if we had that choice. When you're talking about AIDS, though, that "if" is everything.

In December 1996, what it meant to have AIDS changed for millions of people with the approval of a new drug called Invirase (saquinavir). Invirase was the first of a class of drugs known as protease inhibitors, which work in conjunction with another class, the reverse transcriptase inhibitors. AZT and ddI were early reverse transcriptase inhibitors. Basically, they work by disrupting an enzyme that HIV needs in the early stage of the process by which it creates copies of itself. The protease inhibitors do essentially the same job of enzyme disruption but focus on an enzyme crucial to a later stage of duplication. Taken together in a "cocktail" (usually made up of one protease inhibitor and two, three, or four reverse transcriptase inhibitors), these drugs revolutionized AIDS therapy. From 1996, when the new highly active antiretroviral therapy (also known as HAART) became standard treatment, to 1997, deaths from AIDS *dropped* 47 percent. That means that by 1998 there were approximately sixteen thousand people still living who, were it not for HAART, would have been expected to die. For the first time since 1990 AIDS was no longer among the top ten causes of death in the United States, although it still remains so for certain populations, such as African-American children and adolescents. It is the number-one cause of death for African-American adults between the ages of twenty-five and forty-four.

In some adults, the viral load (the amount of virus detectable in the blood and an indication of how quickly the virus is replicating) was reduced by as much as 98 percent. Suddenly, people who were prepared to die got a second chance. As with any powerful drug, HAART had its drawbacks, too. While the regimen produces dramatic reductions in the viral load, it cannot "reach" every virus in the body. Some HIV copies "hide" in areas the drugs don't reach, like the brain, the retina, the lymph nodes, and the testes. Even if a person's viral load drops to zero, he or she still can pass the virus on to another person. The drugs don't always mix well with some of the other medications you might be taking. And these drugs have some peculiar side effects as well, such as unusual fat-distribution patterns. Someone on this therapy might have very thin arms, legs, and face but a large stomach and neck, or a "hump" of fat on the back of the neck. No one yet knows how this change in fat distribution may affect future health. Finally, these drugs, like so many, can be hard on the kidneys, the liver, and other organs.

As with any drug or therapy, you always go on with the understanding that someday you may have to go off suddenly, due to side effects or some sign that the virus is replicating rapidly. For the past few years, Hydeia had had a very good run with AZT. The neurological symptoms had not recurred, and she felt better and was able to do more than she ever had in her life. She had been through so much, Hydeia simply didn't know how to complain. When she got older, she would say, "I don't want to complain. I know it's AIDS, and I know I'm not going to feel good all the time."

You might say that this was a very levelheaded, mature way of coping. For a child with AIDS, however, it could also be dangerous. As I explained to Hydeia, her doctors and I really needed to know any and every time she felt discomfort, pain, or anything that seemed abnormal or different. I know it sounds straightforward, but Hydeia was still a kid, and a surprisingly active one. If she slept in an hour late or her muscles felt a little sore, there always seemed to be a "reasonable" explanation: too much bike riding the day before, staying up too late watching television. One day, though, she was not up and dressed by eleven, which was her usual routine. She needed about fourteen hours of sleep to be at her best, one of the reasons I opted for home schooling. This day she didn't wake up until two in the afternoon. I found her still lying in her bed and asked, "Are you okay? Why are you still in bed?"

"My legs hurt and my stomach hurts," she said. "I think I must have swum too much yesterday."

"What do you mean, it hurts?" I asked, beginning to worry.

"They're just sore, like I swam too much. But they're always sore."

"Always sore? Hydeia, why didn't you tell me?"

"Well, because usually if I go back to sleep and wake up, they feel better."

After that, I started watching her more closely, and I saw the signs. Hydeia took a little bit longer to climb a flight of stairs, and I noticed her not just holding the rail but actually pulling herself up with it. Despite all of her running around and playing, her leg muscles were noticeably soft and, when she sat, a little flabby. Once, when we were visiting a friend, AIDS activist Mary Fisher, Hydeia fell off a stool she was sitting on and just couldn't stop herself. Of course, I knew that one of AZT's side effects could be extensive damage to the heart and skeletal muscles, known as myopathy. When muscles sustain damage, for example from excessive strain or a heart attack, blood levels of an enzyme called creatinine phosphokinase (or CPK) rise.

During our next scheduled visit to NIH, I told the doctor about Hydeia's muscle fatigue and soreness. A blood test confirmed that her CPK levels, which should have been around 12 to 80 (milliunits/ml), were around 3,000. We stopped the AZT, and her CPK counts dropped. Then we tried reintroducing the AZT, but the counts rebounded upward again, to levels that suggested there might be damage to her heart as well. After a series of tests indicated no heart damage, we were relieved. However, it was clear that her good run with AZT was over.

Looking back, I wonder how things might have turned out if Hydeia had begun experiencing the myopathy a year or two earlier, before protease inhibitors. It was as if every time we reached a place where the trail dropped off and we found ourselves standing on the edge of a cliff, science somehow strung a bridge across to the other side. They weren't perfect bridges. And when you started across, you could never be absolutely certain you would make it all the way. But they were there.

Being up at NIH, I had heard the buzz about the new drugs in development. When protease inhibitors were first being studied in children, Patricia qualified for the protocol, but Hydeia did not. The difference between them was that Patricia had been relatively healthy, while Hydeia had developed PCP, neurological problems from the virus crossing into her brain, and other problems that excluded her from the protocol. Ironically, from the beginning, Hydeia had always been "too sick" for regular protocols. The drugs that she did receive at NIH were all obtained under the compassionate-assignment policy. In other words, she didn't qualify to join a study, but her doctors felt that she could benefit from the drug.

This, as I pointed out to several doctors at NIH, made no sense to me. When we first came to NIH, in order to be considered for a study you had to have had at least three opportunistic infections and a T-cell count under 150. Now, here they were touting drugs that might have the power to literally bring children back from the threshold of death, and the pharmaceutical companies (who set the protocols) were excluding from their studies any child who had a history of infections and/or preexisting conditions. Of course, it was important to understand how these new drugs would work for children who were HIV-positive and had not progressed to full-blown AIDS or were in the earliest stages of AIDS. However, when it comes to AIDS treatment, every single case and every single child must be regarded as unique. What works for one or even one million may not work for your child. Furthermore, I knew that the doctors at NIH had learned a tremendous amount about how to treat AIDS from Hydeia, and I knew that if she was given access to the new protease inhibitors, they would learn even more. Unfortunately, barring a miracle, most children who are HIV-positive would, one day, have AIDS.

While I understood, from the scientific point of view, why the study had to be controlled, and, yes, the side effects were largely unknown—until then it had been tested only in animals—it still made no sense to me. Yes, you did need the data for children like Patricia, but you also needed it for children like Hydeia, who had gone through hell a hundred times and were running out of options. After all, I'd ask anyone who would listen, who the heck did they think would be taking these drugs once they got approved anyway? Wouldn't it make sense to have good, reliable data on how they performed in both groups of children?

So I had all of those arguments, but the most compelling one for me was how well Patricia had responded. Within three months of starting ritonavir (Norvir), her viral loads had dropped from somewhere in the millions to zero. Her CD4 counts (one way to measure the number of "helper" T cells) were in the normal range. For most of us, normal is anywhere between 350 and 1,500; Patricia had over 700, the same count that someone who doesn't have HIV might have. At that point Hydeia's CD4 count hovered around 200 (though at one point it had gone as low as 12). Most experts will tell you that anything under 100 sets the stage for massive, potentially fatal opportunistic infection.

When it was clear that the AZT was hurting Hydeia, she switched to a new combination: indinavir (Crixivan), which is a protease inhibitor; and two reverse transcriptase inhibitors (like AZT): ddI, an "old school" drug first approved in 1991, and 3TC (lamivudine, or Epivir), which had been approved in 1995. She seemed to be responding well, and every three weeks or so, NIH would run literally dozens of tests on her blood to track viral activity.

There were many numbers to watch, but the two to concentrate on were the viral load and the T cells. What the numbers mean varies from person to person. For Hydeia, whose viral load had never gone down to zero, anything between 200 and 2,500 was "normal." Even what sounds like a big leap was not necessarily cause for alarm. That is because a blood test is like a snapshot. It reads the viral load at a moment in time. There's no way to be certain, for instance, that someone's range of "normal" viral load is not much lower or much higher than the blood sample shows. Also, increases in viral load can be temporary and inexplicable. Something like a developing cold can cause the numbers to shoot up. Rather than focus on any single test, you have to patiently wait it out over the course of several viral-load results to see if a trend emerges. It is only then that you can make an informed decision about changing medication. If you jumped to make changes every time you saw a fluctuation, you'd risk exhausting most of the available drugs in a very short time. It can be difficult to sit tight after a bad report. Sooner or later, though, you realize that you just can't afford to panic with every blip in the counts. Still, it's never easy.

We were in Detroit when Hydeia's nurse-practitioner at NIH called to give me the latest lab report and make the appointment for Hydeia's next visit in two or three weeks. She told me that Hydeia's viral load was up and that her T cells were down. Of course, this was not good news, but it was all a matter of perspective. Hydeia's T cells had been as low as 12, so while I wasn't happy, there wasn't cause for alarm yet. When the nurse-practitioner said that her viral load was at about 18,000, I thought to myself, *Okay, we'll have to keep an eye on that.* After all, we'd seen Hydeia's viral load shoot up and hover around 80,000 or 90,000 before. In fact, I remember hanging up the telephone wondering why she sounded so concerned.

About two weeks later at NIH Hydeia had more blood drawn for tests. When those results came in, the nurse-practitioner called. "So, how is it?" I asked.

"Oh, *much* better," she replied, sounding relieved. "Her viral load is only at eighty thousand."

"*Only* at eighty thousand?" I asked in a panic. "What do you mean, *only* eighty thousand? Last time, it was just eighteen thousand."

"Pat, the last time we talked, I said *187,000.*"

"Oh, my God!" I exclaimed.

"Well, I was wondering why you sounded so calm," she said. A few years later I could almost laugh about this, but then it was anything but funny, because it signaled the possibility that the virus might be breaking through the new drugs, too. The next blood test showed the viral load up above 80,000. Though it wasn't as spectacular a leap as the 187,000, after a couple more tests, we were clearly seeing a trend. (In Patricia, however, whose viral load has remained at zero for years, that kind of increase would probably signal something very serious.)

Hydeia's doctor suggested that we stop all three drugs and try a new combination. Since Hydeia had been on ddI and 3TC for several years but on the indinavir for only a relatively short time, I asked why we couldn't keep that and change the other two. It sounded logical, but standard practice is to overhaul the entire regimen. Her doctor suggested a new cocktail of Viracept (nelfinavir), Viramune (nevirapine), and d4T (stavudine, Zerit).

Within a few days on the new meds, blood tests revealed that Hydeia had developed what the doctors described as "giant platelets." Platelets are essential to the blood's ability to clot, and it was known that HIV can decrease platelet levels. No one could tell me exactly what "giant platelets" were or what they meant, but this was clearly an alarming development the doctors hadn't seen before. In addition, Hydeia's white cell count dropped and she became neutropenic; in other words, she had lost a significant number of neutrophils, a type of immune cell that engulfs and "eats" invading organisms. This regimen was stopped immediately, and within a few days, Hydeia's platelets and white cell count were back to normal.

While we were heaving a sigh of relief, Hydeia's doctor was

wondering which of the three drugs had caused the problem or if it was the result of using them in combination in a child with Hydeia's history. After all these years at NIH, I understood the importance of collecting data, of trying to understand what was going on. However, when doctors approached me and said that they had never seen this particular side effect before, I couldn't keep my mouth shut. "Of course you've never seen it before, because you don't test these drugs on kids like Hydeia. You test them only on kids who have HIV, so of course, no one knows what to expect when you give them to a kid with full-blown AIDS." Meanwhile, it seemed that every time I opened the newspaper, there was another article about the new "miracle" drugs and how great they were. *Yeah,* I would think, *great for someone who doesn't have AIDS yet.* As you can imagine, I was not in the mood to entertain their proposal that we try to reintroduce the new drugs one at a time. They had run an Internet search of every medical database in the world; as far as they could tell, no one had ever had this type of reaction before. They were understandably curious.

There was a lot of discussion on these points, which I put an end to by saying, "Do I look like I have *stupid* tattooed across my forehead? Here you are telling me that you've never seen this reaction before. You don't know what it means today or what it might mean tomorrow. This time, it looks like we reversed it, but what if on a second trial it gets worse, or it doesn't reverse? Then Hydeia will be left with a preexisting condition that will exclude her from the next drug that might help her. So you are not going to try these drugs again. We're starting fresh, with something else."

The doctor said, "Pat, you really need to calm down."

"Yes, I know," I snapped back. "It's always Pat who needs to calm down."

I suppose that if there hadn't been any other options, we'd have had no choice. However, I knew that there were. As much

as Hydeia and our family had made the commitment to become
a living part of the research, there were limits, too. The other
complicating factor, if that's what you want to call it, was that I
always looked long-term. For me it was not always about what
a certain med could do for Hydeia today but how it would act
over time and what issues it might present tomorrow. Unlike antibiotics, which literally kill bacteria, antivirals at their best can
only "cripple" the virus by interfering in some way with its normal functioning. Even when your viral load hits zero, the virus
is still there, still waiting, with HIV's seemingly infinite capacity
to mutate, or change. HIV is notorious for continually mutating
into forms that are "smarter" and more resistant than its "an-
cestors" to a particular drug. (This ability to mutate presents
one of the major obstacles in the quest for an HIV vaccine.)
Once a resistant form of the virus emerges, it gets busy infecting
healthy cells and "setting up shop" inside them, churning out
millions of copies of the "new and improved"—in other words,
resistant and stronger—version. When this happens, we say that
the virus "broke through" the med.

No matter how well Hydeia or Patricia may be responding to
their current regimen, we always have to think one step ahead.
We always have to assume that one day the virus will break
through and the meds will have to be changed. My strategy is
always to get the longest run out of any drug they take and not
to go switching from one to another simply because the other is
"new" or lacks some minor side effects. Every time you change
drugs, you reduce the pool of future possibilities. Even if there
are fifty available drugs we haven't tried, I always operate on the
assumption that my daughters may not be able to tolerate many
of them. That's why when the buzz about the protease inhibitors
began, I didn't get too excited. I'd seen enough to know that
while a drug might work a miracle in one child or another, there
is no such thing as a "miracle drug" that works equally well for
everyone. I look at Patricia, who has been on AZT for over nine

years with no side effects, and then at Hydeia, whose muscles were being "eaten" by the same drug. It's important to have hope, but you also have to temper it with reality.

Fortunately, Hydeia was able to go back to the indinavir/ddI/ 3TC combination with the addition of IL-2, or interleukin-2, a synthetic version of a substance that prompts immune cells to become active and to reproduce. IL-2 helps patients like Hydeia maintain and even increase their natural levels of CD4 immune cells. No one could tell me why the counts zoomed up or why they fell back down; nobody knew. For all that we know about this virus, it remains inscrutable and unpredictable. There are no simple answers or quick fixes. There is no one who can tell you that everything is going to be all right or that you are making the right decision. You just keep moving, hoping to keep your child always one step ahead of the virus.

SEVEN

*N*ineteen ninety-six was an eventful year, for many reasons. It was the first year in which deaths from AIDS in the United States decreased, thanks to protease-inhibitor therapy. Unfortunately, not all the news was good. People—especially minority women, children, and young adults—were being infected at higher rates than ever before. By 1998, 62 percent of women and 62 percent of children with AIDS were African-American. IV drug use and intimate heterosexual or homosexual contact with an IV drug user were by far the most common routes of transmission. Ironically, these were also the modes of transmission most easily "blocked" by the now familiar precautions everyone should be taking. And so to this day the epidemic rages on.

Between 1996 and 1998, the number of AIDS cases had increased by 16 percent, from approximately 548,000 to 665,000. By 1998 more than 400,000 Americans had died—nearly seven times more than the number of Americans killed in the Vietnam War. Both here in America and around the world, awareness, education, and science were winning some battles but losing the

TO MY VERY SPECIAL FRIENDS WHO I LOST BUT WILL ALWAYS LOVE

It is very hard when you lose someone you love. There were two very special women who have died and who I miss a lot. First there was Elizabeth. Elizabeth was special because she always called me Hydāia. And she was the only person I let do that. She always had a big smile on her face. And she was always happy when she saw me. I think she is happy now because she is with her daughter.

The other woman is Teri. Teri also always had a big, big smile. She screamed a lot. Happy screams. That would always make me laugh. I think that she is happy too because she is with her son. I hope that Elizabeth and Teri are together in Heaven with all my other friends. I hope that they have a good time.

But it still gets harder when I lose someone I know well and love. This is because sometimes I don't understand why I am doing well. It doesn't feel fair. I just want Teri and Elizabeth and all my friends to know that I love them, that one day we will all be together, it is just not my time yet.

Hydeia
Age eleven

war. By 1997, worldwide, nearly 6.5 million people had died of AIDS and an estimated 22 million were infected. By the end of 2000, nearly 22 million people had died and over 36 million were infected.

Despite having lived in AIDS's shadow for nearly a decade, I found it hard to believe that people still needed to be convinced, frightened, nagged, embarrassed, and bullied into taking the threat seriously. My years in social work had taught me that human beings did not always act on logic or common sense. There is a self-protective part inside each of us that reflexively blunts every possible threat with the comfort of believing "It can't happen to me." Today it's nearly impossible to find anyone whose life has not been touched in some way by AIDS. People still put themselves at risk, still get infected, still fall ill, still die. Hydeia's work is far from done.

In August 1996, Hydeia and I were in Washington, D.C., where Hydeia was meeting another little girl with AIDS, Precious Thomas. Precious, who was born in 1991 to a drug-addicted HIV positive mother, was also an adopted child. Her adoptive mother, Rocky Thomas, learned that Precious had AIDS the day before the baby's first birthday party, shortly before the adoption went through. However, that did not deter her. Like me, Rocky believes that there is no shame in AIDS, and she and Precious have worked hard to bring this message to everyone, but particularly the African-American community. Precious, who began speaking out publicly at the age of two, always looked to Hydeia as a role model, and so when it was her turn to have a wish granted by the Make-A-Wish Foundation, she chose to meet Hydeia. Like Hydeia, Precious uses her petite size, soft voice, and childlike charm to powerfully deliver a very grown-up message. The two bonded instantly, and Rocky and I have become good friends.

It was while we were visiting Precious and Rocky that we got a telephone call from Mary Fisher. Mary is one of the most

amazing people I have had the pleasure of meeting on this journey. My children call her Mimi or Aunt Mary. A white woman
from a wealthy family, Mary worked for President Gerald Ford
and then became a network television producer before she was
diagnosed with AIDS in 1991. Mary contracted the virus from
her husband, with whom she had two sons before he died in
1993. Just months after learning that she had AIDS, she established the Family AIDS Network and quickly became one of the
most widely recognized AIDS activists through her public appearances, her books, and her artwork. In addition, Mary has
used her family's position of influence in the national Republican party to argue for tolerance and leadership among a group
whose history regarding AIDS has been, with few exceptions,
deplorable.

Mary had delivered a powerful speech about AIDS at the
1992 Republican National Convention. In it she challenged
the party to "lift the shroud of silence that has been draped over
the issue of HIV/AIDS" and to "recognize that the AIDS virus is
not a political creature." Now, in 1996, she had been invited
again to address the national convention. She called us to invite
Hydeia to appear with her and to address the convention in San
Diego, just a few days later. As Mary explained to us, convention organizers had chosen someone else to appear with her, but
she told them that she wanted Hydeia instead, and they relented.

Of course, being asked to speak at a nationally televised political convention doesn't happen every day. Hydeia looks upon
other AIDS activists as heroes, and so the invitation to appear
with Mary was very special to her. Still, she wasn't as excited as
you might expect. I don't think she quite grasped the occasion's
historical importance, and I didn't try to explain. All I said to
her was, "You need to really think about what you want to say.
There are Democrats and there are Republicans, and they each
have their own agenda. We just have to make sure that whoever
is going to be president has AIDS on his agenda."

Hydeia began writing her speech on the flight to San Diego while I took a nap. When I awoke, I found a reporter from *The Washington Post* interviewing her. She had recognized Hydeia and was asking her about why she was going to the convention. I interrupted her with, "Excuse me, but don't you think that twelve is a little too young for you to be interviewing a child without a parent's permission?" The reporter apologized and sat back down in her seat. Hydeia continued writing.

In San Diego we met up with Mary, her lawyer, and her assistant in her hotel suite. From the moment we entered the hotel, it was obvious that something really big was going on. There were security people everywhere, and it seemed as if the entire city had been taken over by a swarm of politicians, delegates, media people, and anyone else with a stake in the political process. Mary explained that she simply wanted to ask Hydeia a few questions onstage, but when I mentioned that Hydeia had written something, Mary asked to hear it. Hydeia read her short speech, and Mary declared it "perfect."

The day Mary and Hydeia were scheduled to speak, we arrived at the convention center, where I discovered that I did not have security clearance to be in the wings when Hydeia was onstage. At first I was a bit nervous about her being up there on that enormous stage, even with Mary. Whenever I've accompanied her to a speaking engagement, I've always been where she could see me, if only to glance my way and know I was there. I ended up sitting in the audience, up about a level off the floor and to the side, where I could see Hydeia but she couldn't see me. I was far enough away that standing at the podium, beside Mary, in her black jumper and white top, she looked like a little dot. Every few moments I'd catch her scanning the faces in the crowd, looking for me. She wasn't nervous, though. In fact, earlier Mary had asked her if she was, and she'd said no and advised Mary "not to think about it."

Mary delivered a powerful speech, in which she again asked

that the party view AIDS as "a consequence of infection, not immorality." At one point she asked Hydeia if she had a wish. "I'd like to live," Hydeia said simply. "My dream is a little different from others'. I dream of a cure for AIDS." Then Hydeia read her speech: "I can do anything I put my mind to. I'm the next doctor. I'm the next lawyer. I'm the next Maya Angelou. I might even be the first woman president. You can't crush my dreams. I am the future, and I have AIDS. I'm not afraid of anything or anyone. I'm only afraid of my mom when I get a bad report card."

Mary's voice was soft yet strong as she said, "I may lose my own battle with AIDS, but if you would embrace the moral courage tonight and embrace my children when I'm gone, then you and Hydeia and I would have together won a greater battle, because we have achieved integrity." People throughout the crowd were wiping away tears. It was impossible to have been in that room and not been touched. In the end, however, the Republican platform on AIDS remained essentially the same: a conservative call for a cure and not enough in the way of education and prevention.

Many people have asked me why I allowed Hydeia to speak at the Republican National Convention. My answer was always that it isn't about Republicans or Democrats. It's about who needs to hear the message. Among the thousands inside the San Diego Convention Center and the millions watching Mary and Hydeia that night on television, there certainly was a large percentage who would not otherwise have heard their message. There may even have been a good number who wouldn't have given a thought to AIDS, at least not as a basic human health issue. There is no doubt that Hydeia's appearance at the convention made an impression and delivered her message. For me, and for her, that's all that really matters. Within hours of the speech, we were deluged with requests for pictures and interviews. If I had allowed it, Hydeia's words and picture could have been splashed all over the media. Instead, with a few rare exceptions, I didn't even return most of the calls.

In the fall of 1997 Hydeia began attending a regular public school for the first time since we shifted to home schooling a few weeks into first grade.

By the time Hydeia was old enough for fifth grade, I began to have concerns about the quality of education she had been receiving in the home program. When the future seemed so precarious, I was satisfied as long as she was learning to read, write, and do math. When I asked the school district about making sure that Hydeia's curriculum also contained subjects such as history, social studies, and science, I was informed that they "didn't do that" for homebound students. (I subsequently learned that this is a violation of the law.) When Hydeia was ready to enter seventh grade, in the fall of 1997 (she had repeated first grade), Patricia was five. Unlike Hydeia, Patricia had been able to attend nursery school at Reach Out, and we were looking forward to her starting kindergarten, just like other kids. I'm sure part of it comes down to their basic respective personalities, but Hydeia and Patricia have always been near opposites when it came to their independence. Now that Hydeia was growing into a young lady and—dare I say it?—a teenager, I could understand why she wanted to be in school among her peers. Healthwise, at least, for the first time in her life, she was living a more typical life. Our regular visits to NIH were now just every six to eight weeks. It seemed like a good time for her to go back to school.

As Hydeia grew older, I had other concerns as well. Throughout everything, I was always very conscious of the fact that simply by being with me so much, under such unnatural conditions, Hydeia had missed many normal experiences of growing up. Of course, there were the obvious things, like attending school, but

there were the subtler moments, too, of growing away or growing apart, the typical separation experiences that help prepare
both kids and their parents for a future of increasing independence and self-reliance. Needless to say, Hydeia and I missed a
lot of that. Having been a kid myself, I couldn't imagine what
it must have been like for Hydeia to go for long periods when
she couldn't even mutter a forbidden curse word without her
mother hearing it. I was aware of everything she did, everywhere
she went, and everyone she talked to.

Now, as Hydeia considers her life after high school, it's become clear that she has no intention of going anywhere. She
would like to have a career in music, or perhaps become a chef,
but she has not yet felt the need to really leave home. It's not that
I wouldn't be happy to always have her near me. It isn't her way
of thinking about it that bothers me; it's the sense I have that because she has been so sheltered and spent so much time with me,
Hydeia just can't see any other way. Watching Hydeia start to
blossom into young womanhood, I became acutely aware that
one day *she* would be the person the doctors at NIH spoke with,
the person gathering the information, weighing the options, and
making the decisions. As cold as it may sound, I knew I had to
start finding ways to push Hydeia gently out of the nest.

Her returning to school for seventh grade seemed like a step in
the right direction. Hydeia was understandably a bit nervous,
but her enthusiasm easily outweighed her anxiety. I braced myself for what I thought I could expect: ignorant questions about
the safety of others, perhaps some problems with other parents,
teachers, or students who were afraid of HIV and would treat
Hydeia unfairly because of it. Instead, we encountered different
types of problems. For the most part, she could do the work, but
she lacked much of the background knowledge the other students had developed from having had years of a full, well-
rounded curriculum. I could see that she had a lot to master
before she could graduate high school, especially if she planned
to attend college.

In addition, having spent so much of her life with adults and having often been treated more like a peer than a child, Hydeia never learned how to behave like a student. Being an advocate— being direct, outspoken, and unafraid to challenge authority— did not always play as well in the classroom as it did on a stage.

I received many calls from teachers during the year and a half Hydeia was in school; they usually boiled down to her disrupting class by "advocating" for her fellow students in some way. Most parents never teach their children how to advocate effectively, so kids either seethe in silence or respond to a perceived injustice with anger, cursing, or acting out. Hydeia, on the other hand, knew how to state her objections and make her point calmly, firmly, and in beautiful English. None of that, however, disguised a basic lack of appreciation for the authority of teachers. Hydeia is not a disrespectful person, but if she believed that a teacher had treated another student unfairly, she simply could not understand how being a teacher made that okay. So if another student was not called upon, or if the teacher appeared— in Hydeia's eyes—not to be showing respect for a student, or if Hydeia just thought that an assignment was "stupid," she made her feelings known.

Teacher after teacher admitted, "I don't know what to do with her." The problem was that Hydeia would make her logical little speech, and teachers who could handle being insulted and cussed at didn't know how to respond. Not helping the matter, I'm sure, was the fact that once Hydeia made her point, other students would cheer her on. When I'd discuss this with Hydeia, often her answer was, "But you taught me to say when things aren't right," or "You taught me to speak up for what I believe in," and I couldn't argue with that. I had taught her those things. Unfortunately, I had failed to teach her how to turn it off. My telling her to sit on it, can it, button it, et cetera, didn't always get through. When I demanded that her teachers take a firmer hand in reprimanding Hydeia for the behavior they complained about, they often seemed reluctant. After all, Hydeia was a good student and a good person. She was articulate and in many ways wise beyond her years. And, besides, she was this poor little girl with this terrible disease. Of course, no one ever came out and said that to my face, but I sensed it. When one of her teachers gave her a fairly decent grade for what the teacher called a "well-written" essay in which Hydeia criticized both the assignment and the teacher, I just about lost it.

Having been a teenager myself, I also knew that even good students get distracted in their teens. In Hydeia's defense, I have to say that there was nothing in her life experience that could have prepared her for the new challenges and expectations of attending school. She had never wanted for friends, but to find herself suddenly a part of a peer group was a new experience, too. Suddenly I'd catch her on the telephone past the time allowed on school nights—really, just typical young-teenager stuff. It seemed unfair to place Hydeia amid the teenage social whirl while demanding that she work harder academically. I found a computer-based home-learning program that was far superior to anything the district had offered her in-home before. Because she had plenty of friends, I wasn't concerned about her socializing. So far, this has worked out well.

In contrast, Patricia had far fewer problems going to school. Or, I should say, none that she knew about directly. I was amazed, to say the least, when I enrolled Patricia in kindergarten and found myself dealing with the same ignorance Hydeia and I had nine years before. The school asked me for documentation establishing that it was all right for Patricia to attend school. In other words, it was back to the same old unspoken and ignorant "concerns" that had no basis in reality. Years had passed since Hydeia attended public school, and there had been other children with HIV/AIDS since then. You would think the issue had been settled. But no. I had to go through some unnecessary procedural nonsense, but I never doubted that Patricia would be attending public school.

I know that all mothers feel that they are indispensable. You look at your kids, no matter how old they get, and wonder who would take your place if "anything" ever happened. It's funny how we always say "anything" instead of saying what we really fear: if I ever died or became so sick or injured that I could no longer take care of them. As you can imagine, that thought weighs a little heavier when you have a child like Hydeia or Patricia. All through the years, my older children—Kendall, Pepe, Kimmie, and Keisha—had been walking right beside me every step of the way. They knew how to work the pumps, do the meds, watch for the signs that something might be going wrong. They took time out of their own lives to travel with the kids up to NIH and to doctors' appointments. More important, though, they were always there for Hydeia and Patricia, and for me. Looking back, I don't know how we would have done it without them. This has been and always will be a family affair.

Time was passing, and the girls were growing up. I was not only a mother but a grandmother, too, and not fool enough to think I would live forever. I chose not to think about it much, but when I did let myself wonder how things might be for Hydeia and Patricia if I weren't around, there was a good feeling in there, too. After all, for so many years I'd lived with the near certainty that I would survive Hydeia. In an odd way, it felt kind of good to think that she and Patricia could survive me. Even so, I was indispensable, indestructible, and even invincible. Or so I thought.

It happened on December 27, 1999. With the new millennium approaching and people convinced that a Y2K glitch could shut down gas pumps everywhere, we were gassing up at every opportunity. Toward the end of my daily three-mile run, I passed a 7-Eleven and, seeing no cars in line, I rushed home and drove the van back to gas up. At the pump, the machine refused to take my ATM card, and I started walking toward the store. To my left I noticed a red car and kept walking.

The next thing I knew, I was lying on my side, on the cement, raising my head and just opening my eyes. I assumed that I must have been opening the door to the 7-Eleven and gotten hit in the head as someone else pushed it from the other side. I was thinking, *I've got to get up,* when a woman screamed "Stop!" I raised my eyes to see a set of tires coming right toward me. The car lurched as it stopped, but still I wasn't exactly sure what had happened. Then I realized I'd been hit by the car.

The driver had gotten in and backed up without looking behind him. His car hit me with such force that I flew into the air and came down on my left side with my head resting on my outstretched upper arm and my left leg bent as if I were running. As bad as it was, I felt so incredibly lucky. For one thing, all my years of taking care of myself and staying in shape paid off. I had a broken hip and a broken pelvis, but my upper arm absorbed the impact my head might have taken.

As I lay on the ground, people ran toward me. The driver kept repeating, "I'm so sorry. I didn't see you." Now, I was down, but I wasn't out.

"What the hell do you mean you didn't see me?" I yelled at him. "I've got on all-red running clothes! How could you not see me?" I felt a lot of emotions in those early moments, and I wasn't yet fully aware of how extensive my injuries were. At this particular moment I was just plain pissed. How on earth could this happen to me?

Then I noticed that the cellular phone I'd been holding when I was hit was across the parking lot, along with my purse. I asked the guy if he would please go and get them for me. Patricia and Hydeia were home alone, and I had to call and have them get in touch with Kendall. First I called Kimmie on her beeper, but she didn't respond. I must have dialed a dozen other numbers—of family, friends, and neighbors—but no one was home. I did everything I could not to call home, but I had no choice. For the first few moments after I came to, I was in a daze. However, once I realized that I couldn't get up, I knew I was in trouble. When I called home, Hydeia answered.

"Hydeia?" I asked, trying my best to sound calm and in control.

"Yeah? Mommy, is this you?"

"Yes, this is me." Just about then the pain hit, and I remember thinking, *I've never felt anything like this in my life.* It was the kind of pain that knocks the wind out of you. "I've got something to tell you. Now, are you talking to me?"

"Yes," she answered softly.

"So you know I'm alive."

"Yeah."

"I'm fine," I said.

"Okay," she replied, her voice trailing off as if she wasn't sure what to think.

"You need to call Kendall on the job, on three-way, because Mommy has been hit by a car."

"You've been hit by a car!?" I could hear the fear in her voice.

"Yeah, Hydeia, but I'm fine. You're talking to me now, aren't you?"

"Yeah."

"Okay." Hydeia placed the conference call, and while we waited for someone in Kendall's office to find him, I could hear Hydeia breathing quickly.

"Hydeia?" I asked.

"Yeah?" she answered tentatively.

"I'm fine," I said as calmly as I could. Kendall came on the line and said he was on the way to the hospital.

"Okay, let me try to call Kimmie," Hydeia said. "Let me call Daddy." By the time we hung up, she seemed okay.

The emergency medical crew placed me on a stretcher and loaded me into an ambulance. By then whatever shock-induced calm I'd been running on was wearing out. I started to seriously freak and think irrational thoughts along the lines of *How could I possibly get hit by a car? I'm fifty-four years old and never even had a broken bone.* By the time they got me into the ambulance, I was hyperventilating, convinced that this accident was part of some conspiracy against me. Words were exchanged over the driver's initial insistence that I go to a hospital other than University Medical Center. I heard the words "You need to calm down" more than once during the ride. That was the first time it occurred to me that I had absolutely no control of the situation. It was probably the most frightening feeling I'd ever experienced. Little did I know then, that was only the beginning.

I was admitted to the emergency room, where the doctors determined that I had fractured my left hip socket. Initially, it seemed that the best solution was to pin the socket surgically. Assuming I would be operated on that day, the doctors gave me no pain medication and would not let me eat. I was miserable, but pain medication would complicate matters if I had anesthesia, and eating would increase the risk of asphyxiation during surgery. When they realized that the surgeon wouldn't be getting to me for at least another day or two, I got some pain medicine. About two days after I'd been admitted I finally saw the surgeon, and he gave me a choice: I could have surgery, or I could stay off my feet and give the bones a chance to calcify and heal naturally. I was in such excruciating pain that I couldn't imagine being cut, pinned, and stitched back up. Surgery simply was not an option. The surgeon then explained that once I was well enough to leave the hospital, I'd be transferred to a rehabilitation facility for several weeks of intensive physical therapy.

I was angry and depressed, and my whole body hurt like hell. Still, after hearing enough doctors tell me how amazed they were that I had not suffered more extensive injuries or even been killed, I knew there were blessings to be counted. I just couldn't do it right then. Those things I'd always said to other people, like my private mantra whenever things took a wrong turn with Hydeia or Patricia—"It can always be worse"—weren't working.

If you counted all the time I've spent in hospitals with Hydeia, it probably adds up to at least a couple of years. I knew the procedures, and I'd like to have thought that I'd also learned how to talk to doctors, nurses, and technicians. After all, I'm a practical, pretty levelheaded person. Most of the time. But lying in that hospital bed, having to call for help to do literally everything, I wanted to die. Or at least kill someone. Between the discomfort, the bad food, the catheter, the constant pain, and the helplessness, I was powerless, and it frightened me. I couldn't stand the well-meaning but condescending attitude of the hospital staff. And little things really bothered me. Of course, lots of people sent me flowers. While I appreciated the gesture, I have never been able to smell flowers without recalling my father's funeral.

On the second day I woke up with a strange tingling sensation in my left arm. When I told the nurse, she said that I might have damaged my heart when I got hit and/or I might be having a heart attack. The only way to check for heart damage was to run a stress test. Usually, this involves monitoring your heart while you walk on a treadmill. But since I couldn't walk, the stress had to be induced chemically. After they injected the medicine, my heart pounded with such force I thought it would burst through my chest. I became frighteningly short of breath and so hot I felt I was burning up. It was terrifying. Next, doctors injected dye into my veins and took an X ray to look for damage. Everything was fine, except I did have pneumonia from just a few days in bed.

On my third day, I asked Kimmie why Hydeia had not come up to see me. "I don't know what's going on with Hydeia," she said. "She's screaming and acting crazy. She's not helping around the house. She's making everything very hard."

I felt badly for Kimmie. I knew she wanted to make things easier for Hydeia and Patricia. However, we were a family dealing with a crisis. All of my kids needed one another's support and cooperation, and Hydeia was no exception. "She's probably just scared," I said. "This is the first time she's ever seen me sick."

Later I phoned Hydeia at home and said, "I have been in this hospital now for a few days, and I haven't even seen you." She was silent. "Hydeia, are you there?"

"Yes," she said softly.

"Well, what is wrong?" I asked. "Why are you acting up?"

"I don't know!" she cried.

"So how come you haven't been up to see me?"

"Because," she blurted out between sobs, "I don't know if I can handle it."

"Well, what do you think is wrong?"

"I don't know." Her voice trailed off.

"Hydeia, I just have a broken hip. It could be worse. I could be dead. I'm not. I'm fine. Now, you need to come up here."

"I don't know if I can," she said weakly.

Of course, I understood how she felt. Not only was she afraid of losing me, but her experience of seeing people she cared about laid up in hospitals also had to come into play. My understanding the situation, however, didn't change the fact that now I needed her. When gentle persuasion didn't cut it, we got down to brass tacks. "Hydeia, have I been in the hospital with you? For weeks and months?"

"Yes," she answered.

"Okay. If you don't get your little black butt up here, you'd better not let me get out of this hospital. I need to see you, and I need you to help everybody else at home. You have no right to upset them in addition to everything else that's going on."

Later that evening she came to the door of my room, and with one look at me, tears started rolling down her cheeks. In that moment I realized that this accident had a somewhat different meaning for her than for my other children. Of course, they all loved me and cared about me. None of them is ready to see me go anytime soon. The bond between Hydeia and me didn't make me necessarily closer to her than to my other children. However, moments like this made me realize how difficult it was for her to grow up and to grow away from me.

After eight days in the hospital, I started three weeks of intensive rehabilitation at a special facility. Being in rehabilitation is like being in boot camp. The unspoken motto of physical rehab is "Use it or lose it," and the therapists and doctors there are masters at getting people like me out of bed and working hard to heal. We were all awake by six in the morning, in therapy from nine to eleven, and after a lunch break back to work again from one until five. During those hours, there were no visitors, no distractions, no excuses.

By then I was extremely depressed. I'd passed pretty quickly through the "lucky to be alive" phase, and now I was simply miserable. My pain medication made me so nauseous I would throw up every morning. And I was still in a lot of pain, so one morning I figured, *To hell with it,* and skipped my pill. I had been making good progress in therapy, moving my leg through the exercises and doing my "laps" around the therapy room using a walker. The day I didn't take the pill, I got up out of my wheelchair and took about four steps with the walker. I was just thinking, *Hey, I don't need those pills after all,* when it hit me. A searing pain tore through my entire body, taking my breath away. Tears poured from my eyes as I stood paralyzed by pain and grasping the walker with all my strength. The physical therapist ran over asking, "What's wrong? What's wrong?"

"I can't go another step," I managed to say between sobs. She got my chair, pushed it near me, and helped me gently ease back into it.

"I can't believe it. You've been here for a week, and you were doing so well. Did you fall or something?" I shook my head. "Did you take your pain pill?"

"No," I said, feeling foolish. "I didn't take it, because I was in so much pain anyway."

"Well, now you know what pain is," she said, and I would have laughed if I could. The nurse brought my pills, and they put me back in bed for about forty-five minutes to give the medication time to take effect. Then it was right back to therapy as if nothing had happened. I never skipped my pain pills again.

Three weeks later I was home, something I had both looked forward to and dreaded. The idea of being so incapacitated and dependent on strangers was bad enough, but around my kids? I felt like an imposition and a burden. Everything I had to do was a big production, and there was almost nothing I could do for myself. If I wanted to lie down in my bed and pull up the covers, I needed help. I needed assistance for the most basic things, like showering, using the toilet, getting dressed, and so on. I vowed I would do anything it took to get back to normal. The therapist worked with me at home, but that wasn't enough for me. Wherever I was, whatever I was doing, I kept that leg moving. Watching me do my exercises, my kids would ask, "Doesn't that hurt?" I'd say, "Yeah," and keep going. Each week the doctor was amazed at how rapidly I was healing, and after six weeks at home he gave me permission to start putting weight on the left leg, but, he cautioned, I'd still need the walker.

So I came home that day, put the walker behind the door, and "walked"—if you could call it that—unassisted across the living room for the first time in more than two months. My arms were flapping for balance, and I looked like Grandpa on the old TV show *The Real McCoys*. Patricia watched me, then proclaimed, "Oh, Mama, you can walk again! You just have to get the lumps out."

"Yeah," I said, laughing. "That's what I have to do."

After a few more weeks of outpatient therapy, which I attacked with a vengeance, I was done and good as new. I made sure, however, to let everyone know that if I ever got hit by a car again, they had my permission to just shoot me.

Over the years, Hydeia has received numerous awards for her work as an AIDS activist. In addition to the Pediatric AIDS Foundation's A Time for Heroes Award, which has a special meaning for us, she has been recognized by a wide range of organizations. She has received the prestigious Martin Luther King Jr. Drum Major Award, so named for an important speech on leadership entitled "The Drum Major Instinct" that King delivered at his Ebenezer Baptist Church in 1968. Hydeia has also been honored by the American Red Cross, Grandma's House, the Centers for Disease Control, the Frederick Douglass Caring Award, and the AIDS Action Foundation. She was recognized as one of Disney's Millennium Dreamers and received the Pedro Zamora Memorial Award for Youth Advocacy. Her work has been covered by publications ranging from *Weekly Reader* to *People, American Girl* to *POZ,* a magazine for persons with HIV/AIDS. In December 1999 Hydeia was named one of the Ms. Foundation's Top Ten Female Role Models of the Year, along with Venus and Serena Williams, the U.S. Women's World Cup Soccer Team, and Harry Potter creator J. K. Rowling. All this—not to mention a number of Hydeia Broadbent Days in different cities (including Las Vegas, in 1994)—could turn anyone's head, especially a child's. For Hydeia, though, it is still all about getting out the word about AIDS.

In 1999 she received the Essence Award in a nationally televised broadcast. While each award is special and appreciated, this honor was particularly meaningful, placing her in the company of such previous Essence Award winners as civil rights icon Rosa Parks, the Reverend Jesse Jackson, General Colin Powell, Muhammad Ali, Oprah Winfrey, Michael Jordan, and a host of entertainers, including Tina Turner, Denzel Washington, Janet Jackson, and Eddie Murphy, to name a few. And of course, it gave Hydeia another chance to speak to the nation about her cause.

After so many television appearances and speaking engagements, Hydeia had grown up to be quite the pro. Still, this was a very special event, and we all looked forward to meeting her fellow honorees: singer-songwriter Lauryn Hill, rap-gospel star Kirk Franklin, comedian Chris Rock, and the designer-founders of the FUBU clothing company. We had a couple of all-expenses-paid days in New York City at the extremely upscale Royalton Hotel. If you ever want to celebrity-watch, this is the place to do it. Even though by then Loren and I had been separated for several years, he made the trip with us.

For the event, designer Cynthia Taylor Rose (who creates most of the outfits Hydeia wears for appearances and special occasions) made a beautiful long gown in a gold African print with an overlay of gold organza and a brilliant green wrap. With her hair upswept elegantly into a bun, Hydeia looked every inch the poised young lady. The event, which took place at the theater at Madison Square Garden, was cohosted by actress Jada Pinkett Smith and actor-comedian Jamie Foxx, but the actual award presentations were made by various celebrities. Singer Mariah Carey, of whom Hydeia has long been a fan, had asked to introduce Hydeia. I later learned that the issue of AIDS is one particularly close to Mariah's heart, since the disease affects one of her siblings. After a rousing and inspirational performance by Kirk Franklin and his group, it was Hydeia's turn. As Mariah began speaking, the camera turned to Loren, me, and Hydeia, who was sitting to my left. She sat quietly, her eyes downcast as she listened to Mariah talk about the fact that young people of color between ten and twenty-five now made up over 60 percent of the new reported cases of HIV. She spoke with passion about the fact that young women who don't even know they are infected may be passing the virus on to their babies.

"And that's how Hydeia Broadbent became infected," Mariah said. "Despite her sometimes tenuous hold on life, she has found meaning and purpose. The work of this incredible child is now helping others to live longer, healthier lives. A passionate advocate of HIV awareness, Hydeia has lectured at numerous colleges and universities and has appeared on *Oprah, 20/20, Good Morning America,* and many other television shows. She is, in a word, amazing."

I looked over at Hydeia and lightly grasped her chin, and she smiled. Here was my child, my baby, the little girl everyone had once told me wouldn't live to see five. She was strong, beautiful, intelligent, compassionate. Not so different from my other children, and yet, because of the path life had set for her, different from so many others.

The lights dimmed, and a short film about Hydeia began to roll. There were excerpts of interviews with Hydeia, me, and Lori Wiener, our wonderful friend from NIH, as well as clips from various television programs. There was Hydeia at six or seven telling a roomful of adults things they'd probably never dared think of, Hydeia with her steroid-chubby cheeks and baby-doll ringlets, Hydeia on that early NIH tape talking to me about the teacher spraying her face with bleach, Hydeia and me walking down a hallway into Dr. Lisa Bechtel's office. There were so many memories captured in just those few moments. Sitting there, in that beautiful theater, surrounded by some of the most powerful, influential African-Americans, all of that—the pump, the hospital corridors, the meds, the crises—seemed so distant and yet so real I could touch them. And there was Hydeia's voice, closing the segment with, "Take care of yourself, you know, and think about what you do before you do it, because life is choices, and AIDS is a choice disease." The film ended with information about how to contact the Hydeia L. Broadbent Foundation.

Before the lights even came up, people were applauding. The cameras panned the crowd to show Lauryn Hill, Chris Rock, and other celebrities looking somber, some even wiping away tears. Then Mariah said, "Hydeia, your life is a shining example of the unbridled power of the human spirit. It's my honor to present you with the 1999 Essence Award."

Hydeia rose, shot one last look at Loren and me, and made her way down the aisle and up the steps to the stage. Mariah handed her the heavy, pyramid-shaped trophy, in which the Essence logo, an African-American woman, is etched in crystal. Then she stepped back, and Hydeia glanced at her, smiled, and said, "Just me and Mariah!" which had everyone laughing, especially Mariah. The laughter subsided, and Hydeia turned to face the audience.

"When I was diagnosed at three, they told me I wouldn't live to five, and I'm going on fifteen in June. So I have to thank God. I'd also like to thank my family: my brother Kendall, for all the work he has done for the foundation; my brother Paige, for being the best big brother I could have and going to the hospital with me and my mom when she needed him; my sister Kim, for moving back home to help my mom and my little sister and me; my dad, for just being my dad; my mom, because she stopped working to take care of me; my mom and my dad for finding the best doctors that they could. I'd like to thank both of my parents for adopting me, and taking care of me, and loving me."

As the applause filled the room, Hydeia looked up and took a breath, then continued. "I'd like to thank everyone at the Hydeia L. Broadbent Foundation for all of their hard work. I'd like to thank *Essence* for recognizing my work as an AIDS activist. And, please, I just want to say that our black community is dying of AIDS more than any other community. And we need to stop it. And it needs to stop right now. And I don't want kids to go through what I went through, and that's why I do what I do."

Mariah walked to Hydeia's side, and then an escort walked her back down the steps as the entire audience rose to its feet for an extended standing ovation. As Hydeia passed Magic Johnson, he offered her a hug, and she returned to my side looking both relieved and radiant. When the applause faded, the show proceeded with the presentation to Chris Rock. He ascended the steps to great applause, but I think everyone was confused by his somber expression. For a moment he held his award in his outstretched arm as if to say that it didn't belong to him. And then looking out at the crowd, he said that after hearing Hydeia, he could not accept the award and that he wanted to give it to her mother. I sat in my seat stunned. Meanwhile, behind me, comedian Mark Curry, the star of *Hangin' with Mr. Cooper,* was tapping me on the shoulder, whispering, "Go get it! Go get it!"

"I'm not going up there," I whispered back.

"But he's going to give it to you!" Mark replied.

"But he's a comedian," I answered. "If I go up there taking him seriously, he might say, 'Oh, I *should* give it to you, but I'm keeping it for myself.'"

The whole time I'm going back and forth with Mark Curry, who had been friendly to us at the hotel and invited Hydeia to lunch, Chris Rock continued talking about what a wonderful mother I was. I didn't actually believe that he was giving me his award until he came down the stairs from the stage and handed it to me. I rose from my seat, still stunned, and said, "Thank you." So now we have two Essence Awards in our home: Hydeia's and Chris Rock's.

Hydeia's is inscribed: "1999 Essence Award presented to Hydeia L. Broadbent. You have brought your message of hope and encouragement to those living with AIDS while educating young people about the disease and teaching the nation compassion."

That was about two years ago, and much has happened since. But I'm ending my part of the story here, because it's the perfect moment to reflect. Before long, Hydeia—my little baby who wasn't supposed to grow up—will be a grown woman, living her own life and making her own decisions. After what our family endured the first few years following her diagnosis, it is nearly impossible to describe how it feels to be able to say something as simple as "She is growing up." There were so many years when I couldn't allow myself even the luxury of holding that possibility in my heart. Where at one time her education fell behind far more demanding priorities, we are now thinking about careers, for example. We have come a long way.

A recent conversation with an ignorant, hostile mother whose promiscuous son had expressed an interest in Hydeia let me know we still have a long way to go. After doing my best to enlighten this woman, I had to explain to Hydeia that now that she was grown, some boys' parents might not see her as this cute little girl with AIDS but as a threat to their sons' very lives. Hydeia understood, but it was a very hard conversation to have. Yet when I think about it, everything about this journey has been hard, though not without its victories and its rewards.

We have all come a long way, as a family and as individuals. We have weathered the gales and ridden the waves, and we are still here. Such is not the case for many of the friends I've made on this journey. I could write an entire book just about the amazing parents I've met and all that they've taught me about love, faith, and courage. And loss, the page of this story that I have yet to turn and, God willing, may never turn. Fortunately, perhaps, this isn't the kind of book where you can flip the pages and peek ahead. It's probably better that way anyway, since what you would probably find would be blank pages. For better or for worse, the future keeps its secrets. Science, medicine, and people like Hydeia keep writing this story as they go along. For Hydeia and Patricia, and countless others we know, the story does go on.

Now when I go up to NIH and hear parents complaining that they have to spend two or three days there, I smile to myself. If I'm in a certain mood, I'm tempted to say, "You don't know how great this is. You don't know what it's like to have to spend six or eight weeks up here, or have your child run through the few meds they had then, or come up here and discover that some other child you knew, whose mom cried on your shoulder, has died." Then I think back to how I was, and I understand that even though the meds, the treatments, the understanding are all better, they don't change the fact that your child is chronically ill with an incurable disease that continues to outmaneuver us. I know that nothing I can say will bring them any further in their grief or their rage than they are right now. Sometimes the best thing you can do for someone touched by HIV/AIDS is simply to listen.

For those who have managed to elude HIV's deadly grasp, the job is to speak out—often and loudly. The battle against AIDS is nowhere near over. In fact, given the rate of infection in communities of color, among the young and especially among women, the battle has only begun. AIDS declared its war on childhood, motherhood, personhood—humanity—more than twenty years ago. By the time our leaders roused themselves to meet the challenge, HIV had become the molecular equivalent of a stealth bomb, ticking away invisibly and silently until it is too late. To some, the tragedy in Africa may seem too distant, its proportions too great to even imagine. However, one has only to imagine what would be different today here had not the virus been discovered when it was, had we not lived in a nation with the medical and research resources we have. Even as we celebrate the amazing strides we have made in preventing the virus's spread and helping people with HIV live longer, healthier, and happier lives, we must never forget that even these milestones are important but ultimately tiny steps on a road with no end in sight.

There is no cure for AIDS. However, we can work to wipe out the complacency and ignorance that breed it. We can each recognize and make others aware of the fact that it is AIDS that deserves our fear, our distrust, our hatred, not those who have it or those who care for them. We can each resolve to resist complacency, the seductive belief that just because we live in an age of so-called miracle drugs—or just because the media tells us that's the case—we don't have to worry.

I could tell so many stories about children who knew, played with, and were friends with Hydeia and are not here with us today. Some of them even made it to young adulthood, only to be lost to an unforeseen infection or complication. When you think of Hydeia, I ask that you remember them, too. And like Hydeia, I ask you to make choices, not only in your behavior but in how you think about AIDS and what you say about it, to your partner, your family, your children, and your friends. Only then can we hope to write an end to this chapter of human suffering and loss. Only then will we finally defeat this foe.

*E*very year when I celebrate my birthday, it's a special day. I know that most people feel that way about birthdays, but for me each one represents something more than cake and presents. For me it means another year of life doctors told my parents I would never have. The best gift I've ever received is the gift of life.

I believe that God is watching me. I haven't read the Bible, and I don't go to church every Sunday. I don't believe that I have to go to church every Sunday for Him to love me. I've felt His love every day of my life. I don't think of myself as being special. I see myself as a person like anyone else. For the most part, I have the same hopes and fears and concerns any teenager does. I just happen to have been born with AIDS. Even though I don't see myself as special, I do believe that there are certain things I have to do. I believe that there is a reason God gave me the life I have, and that is to make people aware of AIDS. I also think that maybe one reason I'm here is to show people that if you believe, anything is possible.

I have been speaking out about AIDS for almost as long as I can remember. I believe that speaking has helped me to deal with having AIDS. When I'm not onstage or before a camera talking about AIDS, I actually don't think a lot about it. But when I'm writing a speech or actually speaking, I do feel that I'm helping people. The ability to speak from my heart is a gift, and one I am especially proud of. Even though I know that what I'm doing is important, sometimes what it means to an individual person is not always so clear. If I go to a conference or another place

MY MOODS

Happy, sad, lovable and hateable
Afraid, sorry, weird, lonely, and proud

These are my moods
Which come and go
Day after day
Week after week

But still I manage to smile
Even when I want to be left alone

People bug me
All the time
Saying and thinking
I'm someone I'm not
I'm just Hydeia
And I'm going to be Hydeia
And you can't change me
And you won't

So if you need someone to be
Happy all the time
And say the things you want them to
Look somewhere else
Because you got your eyes on
The wrong person

Happy, sad, lovable and hateable
Afraid, sorry, weird, lonely, and proud
These are all me

Hydeia
Age twelve

where there are many people, I may not get to speak personally to many of them. Before and after almost every speech, there are the hours of preparation and travel, and it's not always easy to get all the rest I need. Every once in a while, though, something will happen that reminds—and inspires—me to go on.

When I was ten or eleven, I was speaking on Camp Heartland's Journey of Hope tour. We all rode together in a bus and made stops from New York down to Florida, speaking to different groups about AIDS. When we were in Philadelphia, a local television program called at the last minute to invite some of us on to talk about the Journey of Hope, and I was chosen to go. During the segment, the host took live phone calls from viewers, and one woman called in very excited and emotional. She said that she had been trying to get in touch with me since she'd seen me on *20/20*. At that time she was a young mother-to-be who had just discovered that she was HIV-positive as the result of a rape that took place before she got married. She said she felt depressed, suicidal, and totally hopeless. Then she heard my voice coming through her television and, she said, "It made me think that if you had the courage to go on, I could have the courage, too."

She told me how badly she wanted to meet me, and even though we had only a little time before our tour bus had to leave, she rushed down to the studio. I remember seeing her pushing her baby's stroller with a beautiful smile on her face. When she saw me, she gave me a big hug, and I knew that without even knowing her or knowing I had done so, I had made a difference just by saying what I felt and what I believed. We talked and I got to play with the baby, who was about a year old and, thanks to her mother receiving the right drugs during pregnancy, born HIV-negative.

Every audience is different, but the way I approach any group and what I say has basically stayed the same for the simple reason that AIDS is still around. Even though many things have changed for people with HIV and AIDS, some things are exactly the same. AIDS is still a killer, and it is also something you can protect yourself from getting. I believe that this is an important message for everyone, but especially for young people. I don't want anyone to have to go through what I've been through.

Often I start my speeches by saying, "My name is Hydeia L. Broadbent. I was born with AIDS because my birth mother was an IV drug user who had the virus and passed the virus on to me." I didn't choose to have AIDS. I didn't do anything to get AIDS. I was just born. For me, AIDS has been a way of life even before my parents knew that I had it. I guess that's why I remember so little of what happened to me as a child. It's something that's always been with me. It was my life. Maybe if I'd been healthy before I contracted the virus, or if my mother and family had panicked and lost control every time I had an infection or a crisis, it would be different. Everything about having AIDS that sounds so scary to most people—taking medicine, getting shots, having tests, being sick, sometimes very, very sick—was my everyday life. I really don't remember much of the pain. I don't even remember the time I coded blue and almost died.

I have grown up hearing many of the stories my mother writes about in this book. Part of my being able to live a normal, happy life is, I think, that I've been blessed with not remembering all the bad stuff. I'm sure that those experiences shaped the person I am today. I'm sure that seeing my friends suffer and die at such young ages influenced my activism. But as for actually remembering every detail of these incidents, I just don't. I think that they're all "in there" somewhere, but I don't delve too deeply, because I think that if I did remember it all the same way my mother does, I would probably have a nervous breakdown. Even to think back a little bit is very frightening to me, because the fact is, I still have AIDS. And there are times when I wonder what would happen if I lost my struggle. So for those reasons I find it's better for me to keep looking ahead instead of back. That doesn't mean that those friends mean any less to me. I honor their memory by being who I am, by doing what I do, and by living my life. Because, after all, the whole point of everything I and my family went through was for me to have a chance at life. And not just existing, but living and enjoying life as much as any other person.

These things happened to me, but because I was so young and so protected, I did not experience them in the same way my mother did. Being born with AIDS, I had nothing to compare it with. For my mother and my family, though, it was different. They understood what it meant when the doctors told them that I wouldn't live to be five. It was probably worse for them, because they understood what my future might hold. I will always be thankful to them for protecting me from their fears and anxiety. By their example, they taught me not to be afraid.

What I do remember is being happy and loved and accepted. Sometimes, when I was in the hospital and not feeling well, I would get lost in my imagination or in music, in the songs I'd write in my mind. My parents somehow managed to give me a normal life under very abnormal circumstances. As I grow older, I understand how hard that must have been to do.

In our family we have never felt sorry for ourselves, and I don't think anyone felt sorry for me. They love me, they support me, and I know that whenever I hurt, they all hurt, too. But they allowed me to grow up with dignity and self-respect. They made sure that I thought for myself and knew the importance of standing up for what I believe in. They made sure that I never felt ashamed of having AIDS. That's why I was always surprised when I met children with AIDS who had to keep it secret. In fact, when I first started speaking, it was so that the friends I met from across the country at NIH could go home, wherever they lived, and say, "I have AIDS." I wanted them to be able to have friends and have fun. I wanted everyone everywhere to understand that we have to fight the disease, not the people who have it.

Despite everything, I never grew up feeling that I was different. I sometimes thought that other people were different from me. I have been interviewed many, many times, and I'm always surprised when people ask me about things like my little sister, Patricia. I guess to them the idea that I "found" her and convinced my parents to adopt her is something extraordinary. To me, though, it was just common sense. I love my sister, but we have grown up to be just like any other sisters. We have our good times and our bad times. If we have an argument, we don't stop and think that the other one has AIDS and we shouldn't be fighting. We don't even think about AIDS most of the time in our house. We think about life.

The other thing I'm often asked about is my work as an AIDS activist. Again, this isn't something I sat down and planned to do. It just came naturally to me. It was something I felt I needed to do, and until the virus disappears or there is a cure, it will always be something that I do. I guess one thing I would like people to understand is that you don't have to be a special person to make a difference. When I started, I was just a little girl. No one told me what to say, I just listened to what was in my heart. You just have to believe in what you're doing and find a way to get people to listen. And you can change people's lives, even save people's lives. Anyone can do it.

Finally, people often ask me about death, and I understand why. Sometimes I think it's a strange question. After all, everybody is going to die someday, from something. My mother has a friend who had two sons, one with AIDS and the other uninfected. This woman worried constantly about her son with AIDS, and then one day the other son was killed in a car accident. None of us know when our time will come, not even people who have AIDS. Even though I have had more experience with death because so many of my friends have died, I really don't think about it any more than most people do. Of course, I hope death doesn't come, but I'm not afraid of it. The way I see it, I'm not dying from AIDS, I'm living with it. And that's a very big difference. I say in my speeches that AIDS doesn't have a leash on me. I have a leash on AIDS. By that I mean that even if there are times when AIDS controls my body and how I'm feeling, I try to never let it take over my mind. I have a lot to be thankful for, so I try my best to stay positive. It makes everything so much easier.

I've lost so many friends, and that's sad to think about. I used to tell my mother that I knew I couldn't die because heaven was already full. I'm old enough to understand now that when God wants you to come home, He makes room in heaven, no matter how crowded it is. I don't think about death too much except when someone passes. When I was younger, I thought more about the fact that my friends were free of their suffering. Today, though, I see it a little differently. I feel the loss more because I've lived long enough to understand what some of them missed, and what the people who loved them missed, too. Many of my friends did not get a chance to grow up.

When I think of these friends, it reminds me why what I do is so important. Having lived with AIDS all of my life, I'm still surprised by people who think that it can't happen to them. It can happen to anyone. The sad thing is that it doesn't have to. No matter who you are or how old you are, you can help stop the spread of HIV. Everyone can practice safe sex and make wise choices. We can also help one another by talking about AIDS and not letting it fade from our consciousness. I want parents to talk to their kids today, no matter how young they are. Don't think that your child is not having sex. I want young people to talk to other young people, especially the people they are having sex with. I want people my age and younger—and older, too—to seriously consider abstinence over casual sex or sex outside a committed, serious relationship. I want people everywhere to see AIDS as a disease, not something to be ashamed of. I would like every woman who is pregnant or thinking of becoming pregnant to find out if she's HIV-positive. With the right treatment, almost 98 percent of babies born to infected mothers do not contract the virus. But to get the treatment that's going to save your baby, you need to know your HIV status first.

Before you make that choice for what I call a five-minute thrill, remember what the consequences might be. Lots of people my age talk tough. They act real cool. They think they're invincible, or that they're going to die of something anyway, so what's the difference if it's AIDS. I just want people to stop for a moment and realize that when you make a choice like this, you aren't just choosing for yourself. You may be making a choice for someone you love, or your husband or your wife. You may be making a choice for your future children, or for your parents. No matter how old you are, if you contract HIV, not only your own life but the lives of everyone around you will be changed for many years to come. My mother and I have known of entire families that disappeared because of AIDS. Within my own family, everyone's life is different than it might have been were it not for AIDS.

When I was born, people didn't know much about AIDS. Just a few years before that, doctors thought that children couldn't get AIDS at all. Today we know so much more. I wish that when faced with making tough choices, we would all stop to think about the children. As you have read, it's tough enough loving and caring for a child with AIDS. Imagine how it would feel to know that it was your poor choice that brought the virus into your child's life.

I would like to change the world, but now I'm old enough to realize that I can't. When I stand on a stage and look out into an audience, I know that no matter what I say, there will be some people who won't believe the message applies to them. I know that it isn't always easy to make the right decisions. Even among people close to me, who have seen close-up what it's like to live with AIDS, some have made unwise decisions. At first I couldn't believe it, but now I know that not everyone hears the message the way I wish they would. This used to bother me, but now I know that in the end, people do what they want. The best that I can do is stand before them and talk honestly about my life. I would like to save all of the babies, but if for all my work, there's one fewer baby like me or Patricia, that's a world of difference.

I know people think that because the drugs are now better, they can forget about AIDS. You can't. There is no cure, and having AIDS today is still serious business. I had a friend who was doing really well on protease inhibitors and then suddenly died. So I like to remind everyone not to get too comfortable about AIDS. It's still out there, and unlike people, it does not discriminate. It doesn't care who you are, how much money you've got, or who loves you. It doesn't care about what you know, or what you dream, or how you feel. You can be the best person in the world, someone's brother or sister, mother or father, husband or wife, friend. You can be someone's baby, someone's child. AIDS doesn't care about how much you suffer or who gets left behind. AIDS doesn't care. That's why people have to.

I wish no one would ever get AIDS. But the other part of my message is that if you do, it does not have to mean your life is no longer worth living. You have the power to deal with AIDS the way you want to deal with it. Although a good, positive attitude may not always be easy to hold on to and it can't kill this virus, it can make all the difference in how you feel about yourself and the world. I want to show everyone that the struggle is worth it, that life is for living. AIDS can change a lot of things about your life, but it can't change the person you are inside. You deserve happiness, love, and respect. Don't ever forget that, and don't let anyone try to tell you different. This is still your world, too.

On a more personal note, I'd like to say some things about my mother and my relationship with her. As you have read, there were years when we were together all the time—I mean, 24/7. As I grew older, like all kids, I wanted more independence. Because of all that I'd been through, I was in some ways very mature for my age. Yet because I didn't have a truly normal childhood, I was immature in other ways. Just a year or so ago I felt that I needed to move away as soon as I hit eighteen and be on my own. I love my mother more than I can say, but there were times when I wished I could make more of my own decisions. At the same time, my mother was trying to help me become more independent. I'm not sure I totally understood that, and as a result I began to feel a distance between us. It felt to me that we had lost our connection, maybe because I didn't need her to do the day-to-day things for me as much as I had when I was younger. I don't need to be told to take my meds anymore, for instance. And when I turn eighteen, doctors will be talking to me about my medical decisions, not my mother.

In the summer of 2001 my mother and I both spoke at a National Institute of Mental Health conference. Someone there asked me, "You're almost eighteen. What are you going to do?"

I didn't know what to say, but I sat for a while and thought about what I'd been through and what my mother had been through, too. My mother is someone who not everyone understands, but I think I do. I'm very much like her in a lot of ways. I admire her. She knows what she wants, and she knows how to get it. I guess for years I didn't really give her all the credit she deserved, because I just assumed that what she did for me was what any mother would do for her child. I think that because my mom never let me see the toll those years took on her, and because my mom, to me, is such a strong person, I didn't understand how hard it had been. I know that all parents would like to think that they could have the determination and the energy my mother did if their child were seriously ill, and I know that most of them would try. But I'm not so sure now that everyone could succeed the way my mother has. And for that, I give her so much credit. Of course, I love her. But I like her, too.

All these thoughts were going around in my mind as we sat in the lobby during the conference. I took out a piece of paper and wrote this poem for my mother.

Where will I be when I grow up?
Where will I be with my life?
I seem to ask myself this a lot,
And sometimes I upset myself, when I think of the pain I will cause
If I do not make it in life.
I have been home-schooled most of my life
And under my mother's wing from as far back as I can recall.
My age is seventeen, but my body and mind are not that.
I still have three more years of high school,
And time to let myself grow into the person
God sees fit for me to be.
In the next year, I will be eighteen.
In the eyes of the law, I will no longer be a child,
And to some, this may seem all in order,
Until I take the time to look at my life and really see that
I am someone who is not really ready for that world of being on
    my own.
Family and friends have said and told me that
I need to take more control of my life.
How can I handle something that I am not ready for?
I have always had the fear of not having my mother around when
    I really needed her.
Yes, I have been able to leave her for days at a time,
Knowing I would return to her in due time.
I now know this fear I have inside of me
Is fear of the real world and being on my own.
Her words that she speaks to me

Tell me that I have time to grow.
One day I will be able to have my own life
And do things for myself.
I used to be so ready for that day I was grown and on my own.
Still, in the back of my mind,
Knowing I was still my mother's child,
And as her child, she would not let anything happen to me,
Let me think I could take anything on.
Now I know I am not ready for that world
And should slow my roll
And let my mother raise me the best way she can,
So one day I will be ready for the real world.
With these words, I know I have grown, somewhat, into that
   seventeen-year-old.

When I handed the paper to my mother, she was surprised.
Then she read it, and I could see in her face that she understood. I feel closer to her again, and less impatient about growing up. When I do take control of my own life, I will be ready.

In the meantime, when you think about me, I want you to
think about AIDS. But I also want you to think about me laughing, hanging out with my friends, listening to music, dancing,
and singing. When you think about me, I want you to think
about life, because that's my message, too.

ABOUT THE AUTHORS

PATRICIA BROADBENT has been a long-time advocate for children, having held positions with the Boys Club, the Girls Club, and Campfire Girls, among others. She is a former social worker and a former board member of Members and Advocates for Minority Adoption (MAMA). She is an AIDS activist and a mother of six: Kendall, Paige, Kim, Keisha, Trisha, and Hydeia.

HYDEIA BROADBENT is an internationally known AIDS activist who speaks across the country and has appeared on many television shows, including *Oprah* and *20/20*. In 1999 Hydeia received an Essence Award in recognition of her efforts on behalf of AIDS.

PATRICIA ROMANOWSKI is the coauthor of twenty-three books, including three national bestsellers, the acclaimed *OASIS Guide to Asperger Syndrome,* and *Helping Your Kids Cope with Divorce the Sandcastles Way.* Her credits include cowriting Donny Osmond's *Life Is What You Make It: My Story So Far.*